Suburban Mysticism

A Love Story

R. Scott de Snoo

ISBN-13: 978-0615606569
ISBN-10: 0615606563

DEDICATION

This book is dedicated to my mom who always encouraged creativity, to my sister who taught me I could dance, to all of the readers of the original "Monday Night Musings" who encouraged me to keep writing, and to my wife who encouraged me to publish even when I was content not to.

CONTENTS

ACKNOWLEDGMENTS

I must acknowledge my 9th grade English teacher Lois Wagner for telling me I could write. I am also grateful to my friend Dennis Held for doing my first editing pass and for always reminding me that I'm a writer – even when I forget – and to Pat MacEnulty for completing the final edition.

Special thanks to Milwaukee poet Harvey Taylor for allowing me to include his poem "A Hot Tip." Harvey is still writing poetry, and his books are available at www.harveytaylor.net.

And I need to mention the former president of Religious Science International, Reverend Doctor Candice Becket, who used to thank me for writing the "Monday Night Musings." She told me that she would frequently refer to them for inspiration for her Sunday morning lessons, which really validated for me that I was doing something worthwhile.

FORWARD

My friend leaned across the table, looked me in the eye and said, "This applied spirituality stuff sounds great, but what am I supposed to do when my boss is a jerk, the car is falling apart, the bills are overdue, and the dog throws up on the carpet?

I recognized myself in my friend's question. I recognized us all. I'd worked through many issues, but it seemed that for every problem I solved in my life, a new one was waiting to take its place. I had a big bag of spiritual tricks. I could take the situation at hand, look at it from every angle, compare it to previous experiences, and apply one of my tools. Sometimes I used the ideas I learned in twelve-step recovery programs. Sometimes I applied my own homespun brand of cognitive therapy. Sometimes I turned to the awareness gained in Zen practice. I had shelves and shelves of new-thought books, new-age books, ancient sacred texts and self-help books. I had plenty of answers for all my own challenges, but I didn't know how to pass that on to my friend. There is not a single solution that can be applied to all of life's problems.

I'm a new thought minister. I teach a philosophy based upon the writing of the 20th century American mystic Ernest Holmes. I'm part of a growing spiritual movement that honors the sanctity of all life and respects all spiritual paths while rejecting the dogma that creates divisions between people of faith. I'm supposed to be able to help other people solve their problems. I'm supposed to be able to help people find inner peace. Yet sometimes inner peace eludes me.

One Monday night, I was in a funk. It was nine months since my friend had asked what to do when the boss is a jerk, the car is falling apart, the bills are overdue, and the dog throws up on the carpet.

That particular Monday, I was dealing with some people at work that seemed like they were crazy. I was also exchanging emails with a woman whose neighbor seemed crazy and another whose health-care provider seemed crazy and another whose family seemed crazy and another whose pastor seemed crazy . . . We had a theme going. It was weighing heavily upon me. I sat down at my computer and wrote a few ideas about living in a world that sometimes seemed to be out of its mind. I pasted my ideas into an email, wrote "Monday Night Musings" in the subject line, and sent it to a few church members and friends.

One of the people who read it said that she wished it could be a weekly feature rather than an isolated event. So the next Monday, I again sat down to write. I looked at what was stirring in my heart and spoke to that the best I could. I did the same thing the third week. And by the fourth week, the musings took on a life of their own. I continued this spiritual practice for more than three years, and readership continued to grow every week as people forwarded the messages to friends.

I took some criticism along the way. One reader observed that week-by-week, the musings would sometimes send contradictory messages. Sometimes I wrote that it was important to be detached from life's predicaments. Then the next week, I would say that it is important to be engaged in life's predicaments.

Sometimes I wrote that God is an impersonal power. Other times I wrote that God is a deeply personal presence. I can see how my contradictions might bother people, but I'm okay with them. Life is filled with paradox. The ideas that work in one situation are often completely wrong in another. The trick is to find the right point of view in each moment.

I wrote mostly about my life. But I wrote about more than that. These essays are about applied spirituality. They are about the things we can do when the boss is a jerk, the car is falling apart, the bills are overdue, and the dog throws up on the carpet. They are about life.

I looked into my heart and reported on what was happening there. When I did that, stories emerged, ideas emerged, insights emerged, and the people on my expanding email list responded that I seemed to have a window into their hearts.

The heart connection was what appealed most strongly to my editor, Pat MacEnulty. As she pored through all the musings, she selected the ones that touched her there. What emerged was what she termed a love story—my journey from loneliness to fulfillment through spiritual practices. Writing the "Monday Night Musings" changed my life.

Your life is changing. Maybe some ideas presented here will help you ease through your changes wisely and harmoniously. That is what I want for you. That is what I want for the world—wisdom, harmony, and of course, great love—because we are wonderful. And so it is.

Scott de Snoo

ON BEING IN LOVE

I'm in Love! My heart is bursting with it. I went for a walk tonight, and all I could see all around me was the beauty of Creation. I heard the song of Love in every rustle of every leaf. I saw Love's smile shining in the crescent moon overhead. I felt Love's energy as I watched the men at the park playing soccer in the dark. Everything I see, everything I hear, everything that happens reminds me of my one and only. It's an awesome feeling, yet the seed from which it grew was a feeling of sadness.

You see, I'm not in love right now with a particular somebody. I'm in love with God. And although this is always true, sometimes it's an awareness that slips into the dark corners of my mind, beyond my field of vision, as I busily go about the human tasks of seeking pleasure or recognition or answers to life's mysteries.

Sometimes, my love of God slips out of my awareness simply because things are going well. Sometimes, my love of God is drowned out by the nagging din of annoyances. Sometimes, I'm just too lazy to think about it. But it is always there.

Today, everything went well. I felt prosperous and fulfilled. I received an abundance of good food. I enjoyed many pleasant moments with wonderful people. I laughed with my workmates over some juvenile witticisms. I helped a few people get their computers to cooperate. Traffic was light and moved swiftly. I cannot think of a single thing that I might complain about. In the back of my mind was the awareness that today, October 2nd, is Gandhi's birthday. I don't have many heroes, but Gandhi is one. Remembering him inspired me to be selfless and loving. This is always a good starting point for joyous living. Today it felt wonderful to be alive. Then I experienced sadness.

I was driving home listening to a news show on the radio, and I heard about intense conflict between Palestinians and Jews in Israel. Even among the endless peace talks that sound so simple from my middle-class home 6,000 miles away they still managed to provoke each other. Now there are widespread riots. The news broke my heart. For months, Arab-Israeli peace talks have been headlining the news. Then on the birthday of the man who personified peace in the 20th Century, anything that may have been accomplished in peaceful negotiations was sacrificed to violence.

I am not so naive as to think that there is only one cause to any disagreement, but I know that a contributing factor in this latest eruption of Middle-Eastern conflict is religious differences. That contributed to my sadness. It troubled me to know that we are all children of the same God, yet wars are fought all over the world between people who worship God differently.

The movie "Gandhi" is about the power of peace and the power of truth; these are what Gandhi stood for. As a historical movie, much of it deals with India's conflict between Hindus and Muslims. In one scene Gandhi, played by Ben Kingsley, says, "It does not matter if someone is a Muslim or a Hindu, as long as God is being worshipped."

Gandhi knew the truth. We are all children of the same God. His truth has been shared through books, lectures, newspapers and film. The word is out. And he was not a lone voice in the wilderness. Many prophets, poets, sages and seekers have echoed the same idea. I've echoed it myself many times. But I must be careful to practice what I preach.

The thing that really made me sad today was the awareness of, "But for the grace of God, there go I." In spite of the fact that I often speak about the sanctity of all religions and the unity of all creation, I know that I can be a victim of my own spiritual pride. Just yesterday, I caught myself criticizing the writings of St. Paul. Many times, I've been critical of the fundamentalist Christian church I attended as a child. I've judged them harshly for their intolerance of all other religions, even the other fundamentalists who worshiped across the street. I've been intolerant of their intolerance. And I have to ask myself, "How easy would it be to slip into combative thinking if I lived in a country where I was persecuted for being a New Thought minister?"

Knowing my faults, knowing my spiritual pride, I look at religious conflict around the world and know that I am looking at myself. This evening, the Universe gave me a glimpse into a mirror. There is conflict in the world, and it is in me. And it is bigger than me. And it made me sad. And it made me afraid. And I turned to the only solution that I know: to love God with all my heart.

So tonight, I fell in love . . . again . . . because I had to . . . because there was nothing else for me to do. All the problems of the world stem from a sense of separation, from differences unresolved. The only real solution is to move into a place of unity with all creation, which means unity with God.

To better enjoy being in love, I ventured out to my neighborhood to look into the eyes of my beloved. I walked past homes of Europeans, Arabs, Africans and Hispanics—all people living peacefully as Americans all on the same block. I went past the gas station owned by the East Indian family. I looked in the window of the Vietnamese market. I bought ice cream at the Mexican grocery store, and as I walked home, I silently invited the entire world to take refuge in my heart.

As I walked in love, I realized that we all want to be in love, but we make the mistake of loving in others only the things we want to love. Those are our things. To truly love others, we must be willing to love the things they love about themselves. If they love being Muslims, we must love that about them. If they love reading the books of Saint Paul, we must love that about them too. If they love playing soccer after dark in the park, the only way to honor them is to love them for it.

Many churches end their services with "The Peace Song"—holding hands and singing, "Let there be peace on earth, and let it begin with me." Peace begins when we consciously fall in love with God. God is in all things. All things are in God. We cannot wait for people to change before we love them, because they're not going to do it. They are on their own paths. God is in their paths. Their paths are in God. We simply love them where they are. That is where love begins. That is where peace begins. Gandhi knew it. You and I know it. When we are peaceful and loving, the Universe reflects that love back to us. And it is wonderful. And so are you. And so it is.

WHAT I DON'T KNOW

One of my demons is anxiety. I've always had it. My mother has a theory about it. When I was still in the womb, my father was in Korea for the war. She worried constantly that he would not come home alive. I was born. He came home. Mom stopped worrying. But the anxiety she experienced while I was inside her had by then become part of my chemical composition. This is as good an explanation as any. When I'm not vigilantly watching for it and transforming it into something positive, anxiety will rise in me for no reason at all. But my mind is always trying to create reason, so confused thinking starts hanging thoughts on it—desires or concerns. Then it becomes worry. Worry is counterproductive. Worry creates the very conditions that occupy it.

The best way I've found to stop anxiety and worry is meditation. I use it often. To strengthen my meditation practice, I visit a Zen group. I went this evening. It's wonderful practice. We chant for about twenty minutes, sit in silence for about a half hour, hear a short reading and go home. We chant in Korean. I'm not very good at it. It's kind of fun, making mistakes, trying to keep up. Nobody judges. We just keep chanting away. I don't understand a word of it. For all I know, I could be saying,

"I'm a clueless bozo. My brains are falling out." I don't know.

Most of life is what we don't know. The Kwan Um school of Zen teaches we should contact the "don't know" part of the mind—the mysterious, unfathomable, infinite sea of nothingness or God or whatever you like to call It. If Peter, one of the directors of the center, knew I was trying to explain it to you, he would smile his gentle smile and say, "As soon as you think you know, you've lost it." How's that for an impossible teaching job?

Tonight we sat in meditation with lots of city-street noises just outside: the flow of traffic, loud radios thumping bass, people yelling at each other. Trying to keep my attention off of the noise, trying to stay in my inner silence, I heard my mind say, "So much to not know." I thought it was funny, but I didn't laugh.

Driving home, my anxiety had lifted. I enjoyed the drive in the refuge of non-verbal thought, enjoyed the beauty of life, and enjoyed the beauty of the sunset, until I noticed that was what I was doing. Then, as Peter says will happen, I lost it. Words came back. Oh well. Plenty more "don't know" where that came from.

The words that disturbed my "don't know" mind were lines from a poem I read a long time ago. I don't remember the title. The poet was Michael Finley of Milwaukee. It was a poem about a guy in a bookstore trying to think of what to say to a woman he wanted to meet. Rather than saying something, he stood next to her studying the titles on the backs of books, grasping for inspiration. He was amazed at the diversity of titles and topics. One line I remember is the guy thinking to himself, "The things I don't know could fill a book."

In the poem, the guy never speaks to the woman. He keeps worrying about what he knows, worrying that he is not smart enough or interesting enough. The woman pays for her selections and leaves the store. The last line of the poem said, "Like two ships passing in broad daylight."

Such is life. So often we struggle in the tiny world of the known, standing aloof from the mysteries, the missed opportunities, wanting to know but never finding out. And life sails past. Hmmm.

When I get sucked into the worry place, it's because I think I know something. I'm better off knowing nothing at all. Right now, my rational mind thinks I have to know something—that I have to make this a valuable lesson that will transform your life into the magnificent celebration of God's infinite creative genius we know it truly is. But I don't know how to do that, and that's okay. I'm tired. And tomorrow is a brand new day. And so it is.

THE BIG HUSH

Tonight down at the lakefront, thousands of people gathered to watch "The Big Bang"—the fireworks display at Milwaukee's lakefront. I took the road less traveled by. I drove west to a nice hill and watched the sunset. Weirdness is relative. We all have our reasons. The Big Bang is a humdinger of a fireworks display. I live close enough that I could dodge the traffic by going in on my bicycle. And something in my head was telling me that's exactly what I should do. But I'm growing weary of listening to my head. It is the seat of every bad idea I've ever had. Lately, I've been trying more to listen to my soul. My soul said, "Sunset."

The best sunset-gazing hill I could think of was in Waukesha—in my old neighborhood—the hill I went sledding on as a child. I took a lawn chair and sat in the parking lot of the high school from which I graduated. I had a view overlooking the grade school I attended. I could see trees that I climbed and windows that I broke. I could see roofs of houses where I went to birthday parties. I could see the church where I went to Sunday school.

When the sun was still too high and bright to look at, I gazed around and was flooded with memories. I suppose it was the old church that sent me back in time to Crescent Lake Bible Camp. I went there as a teen. Every year, among the counseling staff, there was a missionary (always a man), who would tell us about his experiences working among indigenous people in wild frontiers. I wasn't very attentive. I only remember one story.

The missionaries were always searching for new opportunities. When they found a population that had not yet been converted to Christianity, they would negotiate with tribal leaders for permission to teach. One African tribe was ruled by a queen. They gave her things like pots and pans and plastic jewelry (imagine). She was a hard sell, so they had to start parting with their personal belongings. In a flash of inspiration, one of the missionaries dug out a mirror, something this tribe had never seen. No one among them knew what he or she looked like. This intrigued the queen. She really wanted to see herself. So they gave her the mirror. She looked upon her face for the very first time, and she smashed the mirror on the ground.

That's all I remember. I didn't listen to the point of the missionary's story, so now I get to make up my own.

The Universe is a mirror to our soul. When my soul called me out to go look at the sunset, it was inviting me to admire its own magnificence. All that the African native queen had ever known of herself was her inner beauty. Living free in the wilderness, she never had to think about how she looked. She only had to think about how she felt. She saw around herself the wonders of creation, the handiwork of God, and she knew she was part of it. She was free of the influences we live with. She didn't have Slim Fast telling her she was too fat. She didn't have Clairol telling her she was too gray. She didn't have Maybeline telling her she was too ugly. Her mirror was the Universe. She didn't have a mirror—as we know mirrors—so she never had to worry about it. When she actually saw an image of her face, it could not compare to the beauty she had always known herself to be.

What do you see when you look in the mirror? For me, it's always different. Sometimes it's ho-hum. Sometimes I think, "When did that happen?" Sometimes I suck in my stomach. But when I'm doing my spiritual work regularly, when I'm really centered, I'll walk past a mirror, catch a glimpse of myself, and my heart leaps with delight. Those are the times that I'm living from the inside out rather than from the outside in—times when I know who I am rather than worrying about how I look.

The Universe is a mirror to our soul. The soul is infinite, unbounded, perfect and beautiful. It recognizes itself in the stars and the moon, in the sun and the sky, in a rainbow, in a lake or a tree or a snowflake. Everyone has had at least one moment in nature when we were so absorbed in the beauty of it, we transcended our sense of self. The same can happen when we are laughing with good friends or enjoying a particular piece of music or art. When we place ourselves among things that are beautiful, the soul recognizes itself. This is what William Blake was writing about in his most famous lines—the opening stanza of "Auguries of Innocence."

To see a World in a Grain of Sand
And a Heaven in a Wild Flower,
Hold Infinity in the palm of your hand
And Eternity in an hour.

The soul is a mirror to the Universe. All things are connected. We are all perfect parts of a greater whole.

I invite you to put this idea to the test. I invite you to schedule yourself a date with a sunset, or a sunrise, or a beautiful piece of music. When you meet it, don't think about it. Just let it happen to you. Know that you are not only the experiencer of your life, you are also experience and the act of experiencing. Become one with the beauty of it. If you really surrender to it, you and the sunset or music or whatever you choose will be like two mirrors, facing each other, reflecting beauty back and forth ad infinitum. If you can achieve just one moment of being swept up in it, unaware of limitations, living fully in the awareness of the beauty of your soul, you will know a mystical moment, a moment of the enlightenment of Buddha, a moment of the illumination of Christ. You will have experienced true religion first hand instead of reading ancient accounts of someone else's religion. You will see the unreliability of the small pieces of painted glass that we call mirrors. You will know how beautiful you truly are. And so it is.

NAVIGATING THE RIVER

Do you ever wonder where you are going?

Most of us have some sort of plan or idea of where we want to go and what we want to do. We map courses, plan timelines, follow the safest routes . . . And when we find ourselves blocked, or going in the wrong direction, we make adjustments as best we can. This all sounds good on paper. It's like all the books and seminars on goal setting and time-management prescribe. But did you ever notice that life finds a way of frustrating those processes that the highly paid authors and speakers guarantee will move us easily along life's highway? I know why.

Life is a natural process.

I know that doesn't sound too profound. I haven't revealed the lost secret of the Universe. But I think it's an idea worth pondering. Here's what I think. I live in the city. All the streets run north and south or east and west. All the intersections are labeled, and all the houses have numbers on them. I can't get lost. I always know exactly where I am. I can plan to go somewhere across town, and if I know the address, I get there quickly and easily. It's simple. And it's not a natural process. It's like drawing a line on a piece of graph paper. Anybody can do it, but it's never going to hang in an art museum.

A few years ago, I visited the cottage of a friend on the Embarrass River. The first day there, she left for the day to go horseback riding with her sister. I can't remember why I stayed behind. Either it was a "no-boys-allowed" outing, or I put on my afraid-of-horses act just to spend some quiet time alone. In any event, it was a beautiful day, so when the women left, I pushed the canoe into the river to take a tour. I'd never been in this river before, and it was years since I'd last been in a canoe.

Being accustomed to the city, I got sort of obsessed with what direction I was going. The river zigged and snaked, and I kept looking at shadows and looking for landmarks to try to keep track of which way I was pointing. I kept trying to keep track of which direction the cabin was. It proved impossible. The sun was directly overhead. I had no idea which way I was headed. It really made me anxious. Then I had a simple realization. I was only going with the flow. The lineal tools of city navigation were not relevant. The river knew where it was going, and all I had to do was stay in the middle.

Suddenly, I awoke to the magnificence around me. There were marshy areas and estuaries where great blue heron stood silent and still, watching the water until it was time to grab their next meal. Small birds darted about, visiting feeding spots and returning to the young in their nests without any concern about addresses or intersections. Large trees all around did what life does. They grew. Some were on hills. Some were beside the water. Some grew right out of the water. None of them complained or worried.

I got the canoe hung up on sandbars a few times. Rather than get upset about it, I accepted it as a gift, an opportunity to stop paddling and enjoy the surroundings. When I didn't want to get stuck, I was just careful to stay in the center—to stay in the flow.

In the spiritual exercise of navigating the canoe, I realized that I had returned to an accurate picture of life.

The city experience that I usually know is artificial, and the model of navigating in straight lines along numbered blocks is merely a convention. It has nothing to do with natural processes. That is why time-management and goal-setting strategies only work on paper. Ralph Waldo Emerson wrote, "Life is a river whose Source is unseen." That Source is God. It is important to remember that. But it is also important to remember the river.

The river of life meanders where it will. It curves and snakes through happy and sad. Sometimes it flows shallow and fast with riffles and rapids. Sometimes it flows slow and abundantly. It has sandbars upon which to rest. If we stay in the center and follow the course, we will get where we are meant to go. If we demand it flow straight, and we always fight to go in a single direction, we will be frustrated because straight lines do not occur in nature.

Don't let life's twists and turns frustrate you. They are normal and natural. They give life its beauty. Enjoy the scenery, even if it is not what you had in mind. Life knows what it is doing because the life we see is the body of God. The life you are living is an expression of God. Remember the Source. Trust it. Remember the river—even if it does not flow the direction you thought it should. It is still flowing. It flows in, as, and through you—because you are wonderful. And so it is.

FEARLESS MEDITATION

My spiritual practice includes meditation. I have a room in my home dedicated to it. I have a cushion on the floor where I sit cross-legged and gently clear my mind. I listen to the whispers of God. Sometimes I close my eyes. Sometimes I stare at a spot on the floor as I was taught by my Zen teacher. Sometimes I burn incense or candles and invent little sacred ceremonies—not to place my power outside of myself, but simply to impress myself with the sacredness of my practice.

Another aspect of my spiritual life is active involvement in a 12-step program. The 12-steps include activities for personal cleansing—inventory steps in which I look closely at my thoughts and behaviors and the results they produce. When I find any that are harmful to me or to others, I bring them into the open, so I can change or discontinue them.

Even with all my efforts, sometimes my spiritual practice needs shaking up. I have to make changes. This past week was one of those times. In spite of all my prayers, and meditations, I still wasn't feeling comfortable with myself. I know that to fully appreciate all of life, I have to fully appreciate all of me, and that appreciation will only follow self-acceptance.

This change that I needed was not going to come from a book. I read enough. I had to find the change inside myself, so I went to the shelves in my basement, and got out a very large mirror that used to be attached to the back of a dresser. I took the mirror to my meditation room and propped it against the wall in front of my cushion.

There is a rumor going around that I am sometimes kind of weird. I'm about to confirm that. A few years ago, my friend Rev. Linda Wise gave a talk entitled "This Stuff Ain't for Sissies." I didn't hear the talk, but the title is etched on my brain. Remembering Linda's warning, I turned on the bright overhead light, took off all of my clothes and sat down facing the mirror.

There I was. Scott facing Scott. Defenseless. I was forced to look at me. I saw my wispy, mussed up, pale hair. I saw my arms, which have always seemed too thin to me. I noticed every scar, every wrinkle. I had to look at my white belly, which looks bloated when I sit. I felt like the toad prince. I looked into my eyes—always too sensitive in bright light—and noticed how my eyelids hang like bags from 45 years of squinting out the sun. This stuff ain't for sissies.

After I adjusted to all I was forcing myself to look at, I focused my gaze on my eyes and began my meditation. Sitting still except for the rise and fall of my belly breathing and an occasional blink, I watched my mind. As each judgment against me arose, I drowned it out with a mental mantra: "Who am I?" on the in breath; "Who is God" on the out breath. I sat that way for forty minutes.

So what was the point of all this? The way I see it, if I can fearlessly look my worst critic in the eye for forty minutes, there is nothing left to fear.

I love the emotional model offered in "A Course in Miracles." It says that there are only two emotions, love and fear. All others are various shades of the two. Love is always constructive. Fear is always destructive. When I sat down upon my cushion in my birthday suit, I was being courageous. But courage is only the ability to act in spite of fear. My goal was fearlessness. If I could fully accept myself just the way I am, I no longer would have to poison my consciousness with the destructive fear of not being good enough.

That first sitting, I didn't succeed in removing all fear, but I made a big dent in it. I've repeated the exercise three times. I will continue until I've learned what compelled me to begin. Perhaps it is to overcome fear. Perhaps it is something greater that I haven't yet recognized.

Meanwhile, I don't expect anybody to do what I do. It is kind of weird. I would invite you though to remember it, and let it inspire you to look a little more closely at who you are. Be alert to self-judgments and self-criticisms you can replace with self-acceptance and affirmations.

Fear is always destructive. Love is always constructive. Spiritual growth means replacing fear with love. Love yourself. You are a perfect expression of the Divine Creative Genius of God. The purpose of all spiritual practice is to grow in that awareness. When you look in the mirror, think about God. When you look into your eyes, think about God. When you look into your heart, replace fear with love. Then go out and have some fun. You deserve it. And so it is.

THOUGHTS ON THOUGHTS ON THOUGHTS ON GOD

Being a New Thought minister tends to invite a lot of questions. People ask me things like, "If everything is perfect, and God is always present, why on earth do I have [a particular negative experience] going on in my life?" They wonder why they still have relationship problems, health concerns or money worries. I also receive questions about the nature of God. I hear from people who are challenging their faith (or mine). I meet a lot of people who are skeptical about anything spiritual. All this is good. I think it is important to ask tough questions. It is important to remain skeptical about everything—whether it is my belief, your belief, or "common knowledge." Skepticism serves us well because it keeps us growing. The only time it works against us is when we pray. For prayer to work, absolute faith in God is essential, but for spiritual growth to occur, we must continually seek new and greater ideas.

Jesus said, "Seek and ye shall find." He did not say, "Here is the whole answer. Now stop looking." Spiritual growth is expansion of consciousness to greater awareness of the Infinite. Our minds are not equipped to understand the Infinite, so the path is an ongoing, never-ending search. My Buddhist friend and teacher Peter says, "As soon as you think you've got it, you've lost it." Keep seeking. A line in the I Ching that grabbed me the other day was, "That which has ceased to grow is close to death." As soon as we think we understand everything, we have committed spiritual suicide.

That being said, I am going to explain God. This is not the last word. Be skeptical of what I say. Look for a better idea. Improve upon my ideas. You can do it. We all have equal access to God. There is always more to be known. Seek and ye shall find.

The premise upon which this attempt to communicate spiritual wisdom depends requires an idea about what God is. This is not a definition of God. To define God is an impossibility. God is the best of the best. Imagine the greatest idea you can have about the infinite, perfect power of creation—imagine the best of the best of the best of the best—and God is infinitely better than that. In New Thought, we believe that God is in everything. It fills the entire Universe with Its supreme, infinite, all-encompassing, transcendent power and love. The Universe is God.

Another way to look at the Universe is that it is made of energy and information. Everything is energy. Sometimes energy is converted to matter. Information applied to energy causes the energy to comply and conform, thus creating all the myriad forms that we perceive using our considerably clumsy and limited sensual apparatus (eyes, ears, nose, etc.). The amount of energy and information in the Universe is constant, and it is constantly rearranging, thus: creation and evolution. God is all energy and information, thus: the Divine Creator.

Now, there are two points upon which all the major religions of the world agree: God is Love, and God is Law. The substance of God is Love, and the action of God is Law—all the laws of nature including, but not limited to, the laws of physics that humankind has identified (as we study within the confines of our limited sensory apparatus).

God creates by acting upon Itself—Law applied to Love. It does this in order to know Itself better. It creates in order to continually discover more of the infinite possibilities that are present as unrealized potential in It. So It expresses as stars and as planets and as butterflies and as ants . . . Each of us is an expression of God. You are you, so God can know the experience of being you. I am me, so God can know the experience of being me. I know you, so God can know the experience of being the relationship between us.

As expressions of God, we are like Gods ourselves. We possess volition, so we can choose the extent to which we want to express our Divine natures. And all of the attributes we express come from the infinite potential of the single Spirit behind all creation. Sometimes we express in pure, perfect harmony with God, but we can also express in ways that run contrary to our original perfect, loving nature. We sometimes arrange the possibilities in self-defeating ways. It's our choice (conscious or unconscious). God is not needy, but within God's potential are all the attributes that can be expressed in just the right (or wrong) combination to produce neediness. God is not mean, but within God's potential are all the attributes that can be arranged to express meanness. God doesn't care what we choose to express. God's love is so pure and complete that God supports us in ALL our choices. We are co-creators with God, so our task is to align our thinking with whatever actions and ideas will produce the greatest experience.

Just a reminder: I'm talking about the infinite and unknowable.

That being said, remember energy and information? I think the most difficult thing for people to fully grasp is that the information that we allow to flow from us in the form of thoughts acts upon the energy that surrounds us and creates our experience according to our beliefs. If we believe, even at an unconscious level, that something bad will happen, we are planting the seed for that bad experience. And if we dwell upon a problem, we are actually nourishing that seed and causing a problem to grow. Watch people around the office or school or family reunion. There are many people who are deeply interested in illness. They don't want to be sick, but they believe in the power of illness. They worry about it. And they can't wait to tell everybody how bad their symptoms are.

I'm always pushing positive thinking. I frequently ask people who are sick what possible emotional component in their lives could be contributing to their susceptibility to the dis-ease that ails them. Knowledge is power. It is the first step to healing. Of course, there are some illnesses and conditions that are beyond our power. Bad things do happen. But we all have more power over our health than most people realize.

A few years ago, a dear friend of mine was having a bout of laryngitis. She was always getting laryngitis. I began my line of questioning, asking where it came from, asking if she was frequently told to shut up as a child. She realized that in her family, going all the way back to her childhood, she was made to believe that what she had to say didn't matter. Her bouts of laryngitis always flared up when she was worrying about asserting herself. Being aware of where it came from, she no longer suffers with it. Now she speaks her mind, which is a good thing because the things she says are wonderful! Tada!

Are you remembering to be skeptical? Just checking. But please remember too that you must suspend your skepticism when you pray. If you doubt when you pray, God responds as much to the doubt as to the prayer. This becomes a difficult balancing act. While remaining skeptical of the things people think they know about God, we must retain absolute faith in God. The Universe responds to all our thoughts, so everything we think, say or do is a prayer. The Universe, God, can't help but respond. So we must look at negative situations in which we find ourselves and try to determine what they mean. Why is it happening? What is to be learned? What is to be gained? What needs to be changed? And what is the best way to make that change?

Perhaps at an unconscious level, or even a conscious level, we've been wondering what it would be like to have the experiences we've been having. When we wonder about things, God reaches into Its infinite bag of tricks and creates an answer: "Here my beloved. It feels a lot like this." Or perhaps we are not receiving an answer but harvesting the fruits of a fear. We create what we think about. If we believe we're trapped, God must respond to that belief (information applied to energy). We feel trapped and God says, "Trapped? Okay. I have an infinity of trapped. Here you go, my darling. Let me know what else you want." The way out begins when we change how we think and how we respond to the situation. The fastest and most effective way out is to take a path that is in harmony with God's nature, so the answer is to Love our way out. Of course we could try to fight our way out, but that would only create more of the same (if not worse).

At first, we must become detached. That is, we must unhinge from our feelings and our egos and step back to a perspective of being witness to the situation. We look at what we're learning. We look at what we're doing. We ask ourselves, "How can I bring more love to this situation?" This is very powerful because God is always waiting for just this question. When asked sincerely, it always generates a new, good idea, and all change, for better or for worse, begins with an idea. We must know for ourselves that our situation is already changed. A good way to do that is through gratitude. Silently offer the situation a blessing such as, "Thank you, my Divine teacher, for helping me to know what I do not want."

Sometimes, it takes several months to create our problems. It's reasonable then to anticipate taking a little time to change them into something better. Although it is possible to create instant solutions, it usually takes some spiritual work. If our situations involve other people, we have to remember that we cannot change them. But we can change how we respond to them, and sometimes our responses influence them. Healthy, intelligent people respond best to persistent, quiet love. And the Universe responds to everything, so for our own best interests, we do well to harbor only loving thoughts.

I know I make it sound too easy and that I'm not where you are. I'm not feeling what you are feeling. But I have used this technique with great success. I have also failed to use this technique and reaped disaster. Sometimes, I just get stuck for a long time, but usually, I am moving, quickly or slowly, to greater realization of Divine possibilities. I always try to remember to do exactly what I've described to you. I consider what I might have thought or done to create the condition in which I find myself. Then I consider how I might bring more love to the situation. I continue to monitor my successes as well as my failures. This is how I grow.

This is what New Thought is about. It is the science of practicing a religion that improves the quality of our lives. It includes experimenting with good ideas.

Keep ideas that yield good results. Discard ideas that yield bad results. Question, question, question. Trust and Love God with all your heart. Pray with absolute faith. These are ideas that make sense to me. And so it is.

NATURAL LAWS

Sometimes, I think I'm exempt from natural laws. I noticed this today. Like many people, I have a job. I do computer support. The building I work in is mainly a call center. Most of the employees spend the whole day taking phone calls. One day recently, two of the employees felt the tingling of an electrical shock coming from their headsets. There was a thunderstorm raging outside. The employees complained. Now we have a new rule* that when there is lightning outside, the call center stops answering the phones. We want to be sure that nobody is going to be injured by the forces of nature. (*This rule was rescinded when we replaced our copper-wire phone trunks with fiber optic connections.)

I heard myself pooh-poohing the new policy. I talk on the phone during electrical storms all the time. Hmmm. How smart is that?

I remember as a child being told by my mother and my grandmother to stay off the phone when there's lightning outside. They explained that the lightning could hit the phone wires and send a surge of electricity into the phone. It could blow my head off. But over the years, I cheated. Sometimes that phone call seemed worth the risk. Nothing bad ever happened. Gradually, I started mentally filing parental wisdom under the broad category, "old wives tales." Why not? Mom and Grandma were old wives. They were the same people who told me Coca Cola and chocolate for breakfast would make me sick. Hah!

I grew up in an age of insulation. With our incredible human ingenuity, we've made it possible to effectively avoid a lot of what happens in the world. I spend the heat of summer in air-conditioned comfort. I spend the cold of winter bundled in Thinsulate or in the nicely heated compartments of home, car and office. I shop at the mall, so I don't even have to step outside to go between stores. I can pull the shades and sleep all day, and then turn on the lights and stay up all night. In many ways, I can temporarily exempt myself from some natural laws, but lightning doesn't know that. It just keeps doing what it always does. It is not impressed by the fact that I have an expensive electronic speakerphone with programmable buttons and automatic redial. It regards phone lines the same way it regards an umbrella on the golf course—just a nice place to strike.

In 1993, we had a summer with lots of rain. Maybe you remember. The rivers in the Midwest rose to their highest levels since people started measuring. Many homes and whole towns along the Mississippi River were flooded. It was the biggest national news story for weeks. A poll done at the time said that more than 20 percent of Americans believed that God was punishing people for their sins. I remember my spiritual teacher saying, "The only sin they're being punished for is building their homes on a flood plain." They thought they were exempt from natural law. Hah!

Throughout the history of civilization, science has identified many natural laws. Some people embraced the knowledge of those discoveries and used it to improve the quality of their lives. Others have kept on doing things in old-fashioned ways, which might sound romantic, but often means enduring hardship or being guided by superstition. The discovery that I believe is our greatest was not first made by scientists. It was the discovery, made by mystics, that we create our experience according to our beliefs—according to our expectations. It's a hard lesson to grasp, and it's a hard theory to prove. I have friends who purport to be too "scientific" to accept it. They only want to believe natural laws that can be measured with a voltmeter or a thermometer or a rain gauge. They don't put any stock in mystics—kind of like me not listening to my grandmother.

A few years ago, I was reading about some breakthroughs in quantum physics. In order to better understand and measure natural laws, physicists created chambers called particle accelerators. They used them to isolate the smallest known particles—the things electrons and protons are made of—particles so tiny that many believe they aren't particles at all but just ripples in the mysterious, undifferentiated stuff of which all things are made. The tiny isolated particles are then "shot" through the accelerator, so the physicists can observe how they behave. Since the particles are too small to actually be seen, observers have to watch their effects. The trick is knowing where to look.

The scientists made rapid progress with these experiments, because they were able to accurately predict what the particles would do. They were always looking in just the right places. After their successes, they went to the physicists' convention to brag. But it turned out that all the physicists doing similar experiments at other particle accelerators had the same experience. Nobody got to claim to be the smartest. Instead they had to compare notes.

That's when it got interesting.

All the groups of researchers predicted what the particles would do, but the predictions were all different. The great discovery was that the behavior of the particles was determined by the expectations of the observers.

To the scientific thinkers among you, I would pose the question: if a particle's path is determined by the expectation of the observer, would the behavior of two particles be determined by the observer's expectation as well? I think it would. And if it is true for two particles, would it be true for ten? Yes? So it would logically follow that an observer's expectation could impact the behavior of a billion trillion jillion particles, too. This, of course, is what the mystics have been saying for ages.

I practice a specific form of affirmative prayer. It is called "spiritual mind treatment." It is a process by which we change our expectations. We change to expect the things we desire. We don't use particle accelerators. We experiment upon billions of trillions of jillions of particles all at the same time. The premise upon which we "treat" or pray or create is a natural law: we alter matter according to our expectations. We train our expectations in order to produce the opportunities, the conditions, and the outcomes we desire.

As I catch myself ignoring natural laws as apparent as the effects of lightning, I have to look at my mind and ask myself what other natural laws I forget to respect. Whether I'm doing spiritual mind treatment or not, I'm always forming expectations. And just as the lightning doesn't care who's on the telephone or who's on the golf course, the particles that are ripples in the mysterious undifferentiated stuff of the Universe don't care what I'm expecting. If I expect hardship, hardship follows. If I expect health, health follows. Living consciously is a lot of work. I have to take responsibility for what I think.

So what about the people on the telephone getting shocks in their ears? They certainly weren't expecting that. Again the answer is natural law. Just because my expectations activate a natural law doesn't mean that other natural laws go away. My beliefs in love and health don't deactivate the laws that produce thunderstorms, or disease, or heartache. Thunderstorms don't deactivate the law of gravity. Gravity does not prevent grass from growing.

I live in an intelligent Universe. I live in it best when I live in it intelligently. When I recognize and respect the natural laws that govern all life, I move into a place of harmony with God. Sometimes, it is time to hang up the phone. Sometimes, it is time to listen to my grandmother's wisdom. And all the time, it is time to be careful of what I am expecting. I can't afford the luxury of a negative thought. Natural laws are always at work. I am not exempt from them. And so it is.

MIRACLE

Recently, I watched the sunset over the grade school I attended as a child. I remembered the first day of kindergarten. My mom cut my hair and buffed me up the night before. In the morning, she helped me into stiff, new clothes, and she marched me three blocks from my home to the school (she never simply strolled anywhere).

I was excited. My sister had been to kindergarten already, and all the reports she brought home were favorable. Mrs. Carlson, the teacher, stood waiting at the classroom door, greeting all the moms dropping off all the kids who were arriving in various degrees of anticipation and dread. Mrs. Carlson had been my mother's kindergarten teacher. She was a veteran. With her keen, practiced eye, she sized up the children and placed them among each other in a pattern integrating the happily adaptable kids with the screamers. She guided me to a table where one boy sat alone wailing his bloody head off. She said to me, "Here Scotty, you can sit with Tommy. Tommy is a nice boy."

Tommy howled for his mom. I remember wondering how Mrs. Carlson knew he was a nice boy. I surmised she must have met him before because that morning at that table, he was nothing but tears, snot and noise. Nowadays, that might upset me. Nowadays, I might feel obliged to try to comfort him. But that day, I was only five. I knew his problem had nothing to do with me, so I got busy playing.

Mrs. Carlson had prepared the room to receive us. Naturally, there were the little child-sized tables and chairs, which immediately impressed me because I had nothing like that at home. Most of the furniture I ever grappled with was built for six-foot freaks. This furniture was comfortable and made sense. But the best part was not the chairs or the tables but what was on the tables. There were huge wooden blocks. There were pieces of heavy string and wooden beads about the size of the hard candy you only see at Christmastime that tastes like raspberry soap. There was paper to draw on and the biggest crayons I had ever seen. It was a treasure trove, and Tommy screamed for his mom. Sheesh.

As I was trying to decide which toy needed attention first, I came upon a small piece of modeling clay. Most interesting! It wasn't supposed to be there among the authorized first-day supplies, but there it was in the box nestled under the crayons. I set to work breaking off small pieces of clay, rolling them on the table and making little clay sticks that resembled toothpicks. I then discovered that these clay toothpicks were just right for plugging the holes in the wooden beads.

I improved about three beads before Tommy got interested. And he got <u>real</u> interested. He stopped crying, wiped his nose on his sleeve, leaned forward, and with one of those cute little beggar smiles only kids can get away with asked, "Whatcha doin'?"

There it was: a miracle. I didn't try to make anything happen. I just got interested in what was before me, and the atmosphere at the table was transformed. That was the beginning of a good friendship that lasted a long time. I did what came naturally, and good simply followed.

To an unpracticed eye, the miracle of the modeling clay may seem like a rather feeble one. That brings me to an important point. We are immersed in miracles. They are all around us. They are inside us. Most of them are very small, but we do well to recognize them anyway. People want to believe in miracles. People want to create miracles. But when people think about the miracles they desire, they tend to jump right to big ones. Everybody wants miracles of love or prosperity or health that are on a scale of Moses parting the Red Sea. We want the winning lottery ticket, love at first sight and the amazing, lose-30-pounds-in-two-weeks diet. But those aren't miracles. Those are accidents. Miracles are created from within, and creating them is an art that requires careful study.

The Supreme Spirit of the Universe endowed us with all the qualities of Itself. As it says in the Bible, we are the image and likeness of God. This doesn't mean God has two legs, two arms and occasional outbreaks of acne. It means that the Creator wanted to enjoy the experience of living in physical form, so It cast an image (us) with all It's attributes. God is creator; therefore, we are creative. Creation is a miracle; therefore, we are miracle makers.

To learn to create big miracles, begin by recognizing the small ones. Electricity is a miracle. Refrigeration is a miracle. The fact that I can write a letter on my computer and send it all over the world in an instant by pushing a few buttons is a miracle. My hands can grasp. That is a miracle. Eyes that see are miracles. Taste is a miracle. Think about it. I can take a little, pink thing the size of a play bead, place it on my tongue and simultaneously detect sugar, raspberry and soap. Next week, I will travel to California in just a few hours. That astounds me. I want you to run with this idea. The more you can sense the miraculous in every moment, the more powerful you will find you become. As the miracles of everyday life become apparent, we develop a consciousness through which greater miracles can flow. The consciousness of the miraculous can grow, but creating the big miracles without learning to recognize the small ones is like trying to write a novel without first learning the alphabet.

My invitation to you is to create something today while being mindful of the small miracles involved. You don't have to go buy modeling clay, and you don't have to write a book. Just pay attention when you do the things you would do anyway. If you make a spaghetti dinner, think about all the small miracles involved—that those hard little sticks that are just the right size for plugging holes in beads were once amber waves of grain, and when you boil them, they turn soft and wormy and edible. Who comes up with this stuff? Life is amazing. And so are you. And so it is.

LEARNING TO DANCE

I'm in a peculiar mood. I'm re-adjusting to myself. For the past six weeks, I've been sharing my home with a friend and her 10-year-old niece. Saturday, they moved into their new home. Before they left, I was anticipating how nice it would feel to have my space back. I looked forward to the silence and simplicity of not having to share or compromise. I looked forward to taking the beds out of my living room.

Sunday was my first full day without them, and I was climbing the walls. I'd grown accustomed to being greeted as I walked in the door, accustomed to sharing moods, ideas and achievements of the day, accustomed to having to tune out little parent-child squabbles as I tried to concentrate on studying or writing. I'd gotten used to having to wait my turn to use the bathroom or the telephone. I'd gotten used to being surprised when I opened the refrigerator door—Snickers, Coca-Cola and turkey dogs were not things I would have put there myself. Then suddenly, the variables were gone, and my life seemed less interesting.

I've spent today getting reacquainted with my self, getting interested once again in what is inside me. Fortunately, I was still there, right where I'd left me. I had to dig out and dust off the tools I use for coping with myself. I had to ask myself, "What makes me happy?" And fortunately, I still knew the answer: I make me happy.

When my friends were here, I found joy in making jokes, sharing meals, finding suitable entertainments for a 10-year-old in what is mainly a stuffy bookish bachelor pad. But it wasn't my friends that made me happy. I made me happy, in the way I responded to them. I could have just as easily made myself miserable by entertaining notions of being inconvenienced or intruded upon. But life's too short to resent having friends around.

A few months ago, I read an article that invited me to think back upon my life and recall the most wonderful experience I'd ever had. My mind sailed around the world, visiting all the places I've been, seeing all the sights I've seen. I flipped through my mental calendar, stopping at all of the milestone events that I use to sort out my life. I recalled graduations and girlfriends, homes and jobs. My mind finally stopped in the basement of the home in Waukesha, Wisconsin where I grew up. October 28th, 1966, I was 11 years old. We had a party.

It was my mother's idea. I was in 7th grade. My sister was in 8th. My mom asked us if we wanted to have a Halloween party. My sister went right off the charts. She had a lot of friends. Unlike her little brother, she was a very social person. She immediately named about twenty people she wanted to invite. I thought of three.

The party was on a Friday night. While my sister and I were at school, my mother transformed the basement. She took down her clotheslines and put up strings of Christmas lights. She pushed her old, wringer washing machine out of sight under the stairs. She cleared off the little work bench that was normally reserved for my chemistry set, covered it with a cloth, and set up the family stereo—the suit-case kind with a speaker in the removable lid. She ran orange and black crepe-paper streamers, set out bowls of pretzels and chips and tubs of ice cubes with cans of soda. To me, it looked like a ballroom. Even my sister, who was sort of fussy, was delighted.

When our guests arrived, my mother went upstairs and left us alone. My sister suddenly felt grown-up and popular. She was shining. Most of her friends were from a youth drama club she belonged to, so there was very little shyness or inhibition. The stereo-record albums started playing. The kids started dancing. Laughter echoed off the concrete-block walls.

I was pleased and amused by it all as I watched from the corner with my little cluster of socially inept friends. We were pre-teens. Rather than risk being thought fools by showing our inability to dance, we made sarcastic observations.

Then a miracle occurred. My sister came over and asked us why we weren't dancing. That was the miracle: she was pleasant to us, and she wanted us to have fun. It was unreal. Normally, she would have been kind of sister-snotty and called me names. But she was having the time of her life, and not even her little brother could ruin it for her.

It was then that I really noticed that none of the kids who were dancing were doing so with any particular skill. They were mostly just flailing around, and they all looked very, very happy. I jumped in and started flailing too. I could flail as good as anyone. We danced until midnight to the Mamas and the Papas, the Monkees, the Boxtops, Moby Grape . . .

The youngest of my sister's friends was Donna Putnam. She was my age. She had lots of long, curly red hair—even her eyelashes were red—and I danced with her a lot. I still have a crush on the memory of her, and I hope right now she is with someone who finds her as beautiful as she was to me that night.

The next day, I had to clean the basement. I didn't mind. Normally on a Saturday in 1966, I would have strapped on my shoulder holster to go out to play "The Man From UNCLE." I was Napoleon Solo, since my best friend was always Illya Kuryakin. But suddenly, my life had changed. Suddenly, I was happy being me. I felt socially capable. I felt mature and attractive. I felt like I was a friend to my sister for the first time in years. I felt like I knew how to dance.

As I was cleaning, I relived the party. I put the Mamas and the Papas on the record player, and I swept the floor singing along with their rendition of "Do You Wanna Dance." As I cleaned, my sister was in her room right above me with Evelyn Whitney hashing over what a smashing success the party had been. When they heard me singing, they put their ears to the floor. My sister said she laughed. But she told me Evelyn didn't laugh. Evelyn thought I was cool.

Now I wonder how, at 11 years old, I could be happy cleaning up the day after the party. Wasn't the happiness in the party itself? The truth is, it was not. It was inside me. The reason I was happy cleaning up afterward was that I was grateful.

Tonight in my peculiar mood, I am asking myself a few questions. Am I going to return to the familiar happiness-inside-me of sitting in my stuffy bachelor pad with my books, or has my life changed as a result of having roommates? Have I discovered that a little risk and inconvenience make it easier for me to access my joy? Am I going to get up and dance or sit back and watch?

My life, like yours, is an expression of God. That means the attributes of God are inside me. One of them is joy. I can access that joy at any time in the way I respond to life. I can get up and dance, or I can sit in the corner and watch. I can invite people into my life, or I can sit home alone. It's all good, as long as I remember that the way I respond to it is up to me.

Tonight I will respond to my peculiar mood by being grateful. I am grateful I had friends stay with me, and I am grateful they're not here now. I am grateful they will visit me soon. I am grateful I can dance. I am grateful for my mom and my sister. I am grateful for Donna Putnam,

Evelyn Whitney, and "The Man from UNCLE." And to be sure, I am grateful that I have you to share my thoughts and feelings with—because you are wonderful. And so it is.

THE TEACHER ON THE HIGHWAY

I'm thinking about mindfulness.

I have some minister friends who do a lot of work with kids. They have a little parlor trick they perform as needed. They can pick up any ordinary item, start talking about it and turn it into a spiritual lesson. It's a handy skill for them. Kids like to be entertained, and mouthfuls of theological theory don't quite cut it. But things in the room, things that are colorful, useful or a little mysterious—pieces of yarn, scissors, rings of keys—give them something to look at or touch. No matter what you hand my minister friends, the marvelous magicians of spiritual stories, a beautiful lesson emerges.

It almost looks like sleight of hand. The casual observer might wonder how Sue or Bob got from glue stick to God so effortlessly. I'll tell you the secret: God is in everything. Everything we see, hear or touch is an expression of God; therefore anything we allow ourselves to "listen" to reveals another of God's infinite attributes. That's why I'm thinking about mindfulness.

I see much suffering in the world. Sometimes, I experience it. It's all God talking. Among the attributes of God is that It never shuts up. Mindfulness is paying attention to God's whispers. I don't always do that. It is always a mistake not to. God guides. I don't listen, so

God turns up the volume. If I still don't listen, God turns up the volume more. God's capacity to turn up the volume far exceeds my ability to not listen. And sometimes, when God gets loud, things get ugly. That is when I start to feel pain. Sometimes, it is physical. Sometimes it is emotional. Many times, it is both.

Yesterday, as usual, God spoke to me. I was driving my pick-up truck home from church. I was a few miles away from home, approaching the end of the freeway spur that leads into my neighborhood. I was looking forward to my customary after-church nap. I saw a man walking along the freeway median. He had a thumb up for a ride. He was dressed nicely. He didn't have a backpack. He was headed into town rather than out, so I surmised he must have had car trouble. I just finished giving a 35-minute talk about listening to God and practicing compassion. My inner voice said, "Practice what you preach." I stopped to pick him up.

The man was very polite and grateful, but he was terribly anxious. He had run out of gas less than a mile away from the gas station. To me, this seemed like no great shakes. The sun was shining. The air was about 70 degrees. If it had been me, I would have laughed at myself and enjoyed the walk. But as I said, this guy was anxious. To him, this was a major crisis because he had run out of gas on the way to church. He told me he knew that it was Satan trying to keep him from going. That scared him. He was certain that he would be in a losing battle with the Lord of Darkness if he didn't get to the safety of God's house.

I did not try to "save" him with Religious Science platitudes. He did not need to hear me say that God is everywhere at all times. He did not need to hear me say that Satan is merely a metaphor for erroneous thinking. He needed to get to the safety of his spiritual community. He needed to connect to God in the way that he understands connecting to God. I did my best to sooth him. I told him I would help him get on his way. I told him I was coming from church myself.

He saw my suit and my briefcase and my baskets and asked if I was a minister. I said, "Yea." That's all I said. We were already pulling into the gas station. The man ran inside, bought a gas can, pumped two gallons of gas in it and was back in my truck faster than I could imagine was possible. I do things slowly. This guy was not fooling around.

As we drove the short distance toward his car, he seemed to calm down. He muttered a little bit more about the devil, and then he said to me, "Nobody would stop to help me. Then I said a prayer, and there you were."

I said, "Isn't it interesting how that works?"

He said, "Yea. God is good. God is so good." He said this emphatically—with all his heart and soul. I suddenly had one of those mystical moments. I almost burst into tears. What he said and the way he said it were so very true. Suddenly he was my minister. I knew I must learn to throw myself upon the power of God with fervor like his.

When we got to his car, he had a little bit of trouble getting the gas in the tank. He was still frantic to be in the safety of his church, and as he tried to hold his license plate down and get the plastic nozzle of his gas can through the little spring-loaded opening of the gas tank, he spilled gas on his hands and on his shoes. I reached down and held the gas-soaked license plate out of the way. He was then able to manipulate the spout, and he succeeded in getting the gasoline where it was supposed to be. He said, "I'm going to go to church smelling like gas, but I don't care."

He saved a few drops of gas, which he poured into the carburetor to prime it. He thanked me about twenty times as he jumped into the car and started it up. He told me his name is Louis. I told him my name is Scott. He sped off to church—to be with God. I went to my house—to be with God.

I looked at the clock as I walked in the door. I was home at my regular time. This whole short adventure didn't affect my routine at all, but it gave me something to think about.

I'm glad I do not share Louis's belief that there is a devil sneaking around trying to get me. I'm glad I know God as the One and Only Source and Substance of All Creation. I'm happy with my beliefs. But I also recognize that Louis's belief in the devil is serving him in a way that I need to serve myself. At the first sign of trouble, Louis feels the presence of Satan and frantically rushes to get back to God. He knows that if he doesn't, Satan will get his hooks in, and the problem will get worse. That's the lesson.

I know that all my problems are my own creations, so I somehow feel it's okay to dally with them. When I have an erroneous thought, the Power of the Universe responds by creating a corresponding condition. And I sit and look at it. I feel my feelings, grieve a little, make a mental note to pray and meditate . . . later, maybe after I take a nap or a shower or have something to eat. That is bad thinking! It is missing the whole point of spiritual living and the practice of scientific prayer. If I truly want to create the life I desire, if I really want to experience love, prosperity, health and creative self-expression all the time, I have to practice what I preach in every moment of every situation.

Little problems that make me feel a little bit uncomfortable are the whispers of God. God wants to be heard. God will get louder if I ignore It. All of the big problems that I create began as little problems. If at the slightest stirring of negativity, I would frantically run back to God, I could avoid the hooks that hold me in my problems. By correct action, I could escape the effects of the "Law of Growth" that works just as surely on a bad idea as on a good one.

That is why I'm thinking about mindfulness. That is why I'm looking for the spiritual lesson in everything that I touch. When I pick up a piece of yarn, I can think about the beautiful way God binds all things together. When I pick up a scissors, I can think about how God allows me to trim away rough edges and shape my life to my pleasing. When I pick up my keys, I can remember how spiritual practice unlocks my heart and opens me to receive the gifts of Spirit. When I look for God in all things, I attune myself to seeing God in all my thoughts and feelings. Then when I see a thought or feeling that is out of harmony with my higher good, I can run frantically to the safety and security of the One and Only Perfect Source of all that is and will ever be.

This week, I'm thinking about mindfulness. As always, I invite you to join me in knowing a greater truth. We can do this by looking for God in all things; we can do this by running back to God at the first stirring of negativity. We can know what Louis knows. Maybe we know it in a different way, but it's the same principle, the same stuff, the same God. Thank you, Louis. Thank you, God. And so it is.

THE CENTER OF THE UNIVERSE

What if I'm the center of the Universe? I mean, what if it's all about Me? Have you ever wondered, what if everything is mine, all mine? What if I am the reason for it all? What if I am God?

What if everything is just the way it is because I have made it so? It would mean that everyone treats me just the way they do because I have invited them, or trained them, to treat me just that way. It would mean that I have everything I have because that is what I chose to create. It would mean that the world looks just the way it does because all of the things I've thought and said and done up until now have been designing a template through which creation occurs. What if I am responsible—or to blame—for the world as it is?

I realize this is a far-fetched idea for most people. It may even make some people nervous. To them, it may sound blasphemous to ask, "What if I am God?" But as far as I know, no sacred text of any religion has a commandment that forbids pondering enormous philosophical questions. I'm not declaring myself the Divine Creator. I wouldn't want to answer all the requests that would come out of that. Can you imagine? "Please Mr. GodScott, may I win the lottery this week?" —"Oh, um. Sorry. I already promised it to Edith." Who needs that? Not me. I'm just wondering, "What if?"

There was a time when this question would never have crossed my mind. It was a time when I actually thought that I WAS the center of the Universe. I was a little kid, and within the Universe of my awareness, all the evidence I had said I was It. I even remember the first experience I had that suggested perhaps I was not.

I grew up in a charming little house in a charming little neighborhood. My grandparents lived close by, and there was a path between my house and their house, which I traveled freely. That was my Universe. I was an adorable kid with curly red hair and freckles, and my parents and grandparents, even my sister who was also adorable but a little bit older, all doted upon me and fulfilled my every need. If I wanted something I couldn't have, they were masters at redirecting my interest to something else, so it felt as if all my desires were being fulfilled. And I was the center of attention. All I had to do was be there, and everyone made a fuss over how wonderful I was.

One day, I was in my grandparents' living room. I was probably four years old. It was the safest, most nurturing place in my world with my grandpa's brown chair, my grandma's Hammond organ and the long, pink couch that grandma always called the davenport. I was playing happily when company arrived. They were my grandparents' best friends. I sat expecting they would come straight to me and express their admiration. The way I understood things, that was the drill. It never occurred to me that anyone would have any higher priority than that. But it didn't happen. It was as if I was invisible. The grown-ups only paid attention to each other. Even though I'd never had this problem before, I had an ace up my sleeve. I'd recently learned how to turn a somersault, and it never failed to draw adoring praise. I tucked and rolled. Nothing. I turned around and rolled back to where I started. Still nothing. I tried a few more times, but I already knew I'd lost my audience. My career as   Center-of-the-Universe   was   over.

It was all downhill from there. A few short years later, I was in school, where the teacher had to divide her attention among a few dozen of us, and every kid had a different agenda and a different routine. I was not rewarded for standing out but instead for fitting in. Conformity was a goal, and in conformity is mediocrity. I felt like part of the herd.

But what if it was all a mistake? What if I am the center of it all? What if I created the herd just so I could be part of it? Suppose that day I was turning somersaults at my grandparents' house, the routine flopped because I was using old material. They'd all seen the somersault. Maybe it was time to whistle, or perhaps to stand on one foot. What if I've been the center of everything all along, but I failed to capitalize on it because I've been stuck doing old routines, thinking old thoughts and not looking ahead to something greater? What if I am God?

If I am, it would mean that I created all this. It would mean that every extra ounce of fat on my body is there because I put it there. It would mean that every scar I have, every ache or pain I feel, is the result of a choice I've made along the way. It would also mean that all the people who are in my life are there because I have invited them in. Everyone who isn't there doesn't call or visit because I have not invited them to. Every rejection I've ever experienced was a result of something I chose to say or do (or not say or do).

If I'm the center of the Universe, I live where I live because that is what I have chosen. My bank account contains only the amount that I have chosen to put there. My income is what I have settled for. My career is what I elected to do. I am not a movie star because I have not chosen to be a movie star. I am not the president because I chose somebody else to do the job for me. If I'm the center of the Universe, then I am responsible for my life and how I fit into everything.

If I am responsible, then I must look at what I don't like and begin to take the necessary actions to change it. This would require new ideas. It would mean that I would have to stop turning somersaults and try whistling or standing on one foot. I would have to recognize that I am the only authority in my life. I would have to watch my every thought, word and deed to make sure that it is creating what I want to create. I would have to live consciously in every moment to avoid creating the things I don't want. I would have to live intelligently. Hmm.

About ten years ago, all the motivational speakers had a line that went, "Live each day as if it were your last." I'm not sure it was really sage advice. I know many people who would take it as an excuse to get drunk. But it doesn't matter. I haven't heard it in awhile. The motivational speakers have apparently moved on to something new. But the other day I heard a comedian on the radio say, "I try to live each day as if it were my last. I get up, spend about three hours making funeral arrangements, then I sit and wait for it to end."

I have a different idea—a new idea. What if I live each day as if I were God? What if I live each moment as if I were responsible for everything? I would have to decide exactly what I want my life to look like. I would have to make choices that support my ideals and avoid creating anything that might run counter to what I want the world, my world, to look like.

So that's the message. Live each day as if you were God. What have you got to lose? And you might discover that you are! And so it is.

A HOT TIP

Right now—in this moment—I'm at peace with myself just as I am. This is not always true, but I've been this way for over a week. It started when I went on a trip last Sunday. I left my house with that over-anxious feeling that comes from being focused on my destination. I caught it early. I was driving to the airport all alone, and heard myself, for no particular reason, rattle off a rapid-fire string of my favorite cuss words. This is always a reliable indicator that I have turned off my spiritual practice and let the 10,000 idiots run loose in my brain.

I spent the next hour or so shifting my focus—bringing my mind back to each moment rather than worrying about where I was not. So when I got to the airport in Chicago and learned that my flight had been canceled because of high winds, I was able to say to myself, "So what? It doesn't make me any less on vacation." I decided that if the creative intelligence of the Universe needed to have me spend the first six hours of my vacation at O'Hare Airport, I was going to enjoy every minute of it.

I walked around the airport and shopped. I looked at neckties and briefcases, but I already have too many of those. I thought about getting a massage, but I wasn't tense. I eventually had a meal at Chili's. Then I bought a coffee drink from Starbuck's. As I walked around sipping it, I thought I should share my good spirits. Many people were stranded, so I tried to comfort them by smiling or striking up conversation.

Most of the people I encountered thought I was loony. When I smiled or spoke, they would cast their gazes to the floor and scurry past me as quickly as they could. I wasn't surprised. I get this same reaction from people in the mall at Christmastime. It's not that people don't want to be nice. It's not that they don't want to make new friends. But they are afraid, and I think there are two main reasons why. For many, a smile from someone they don't know triggers an inner instruction that was imprinted many years ago. I smile, and from inside their heads, they hear their mothers' commandment: "Don't talk to strangers." This was very good advice when they were children walking to and from school, but they've internalized it so deeply, they overlook the fact that now in their forties, they can assess for themselves who is dangerous and who is not.

I believe the second reason that people have trouble making eye contact is shame. I think people are filled with it. I believe this because it is something I found within myself. As I was trying to embark upon my spiritual journey, and I had gotten my life into pretty good order, I discovered that I could be functioning just fine one minute, and be filled with dread the next. The dread was that I might be found out—that somebody might see inside my black heart and know the terrible things I had done. But the terrible things that were torturing me were mostly old memories from my childhood—forgotten by everyone except me.

There was a time I gave a foolish answer to a question in school, and all of the other children laughed, and the time my best friend's mother caught me going potty beside the garage. These were not serious crimes. There were worse things. There was the time I hit Eddie Marshman in the eye with a snowball. I had layers of shame to go with that one. I hardly knew Eddie. He went to my school. I knew his name. That's about it. He was a harmless boy, but I chose to make him my enemy. I think it was because he had red hair.

You see, my hair was red—bright and curly—and I hated it. Other children teased me and called me "carrot top." I was angry, and when I looked at Eddie Marshman, I saw something I hated about myself. So one day walking to school, with neither reason nor provocation, I scooped up a mitten full of snow, packed it into a ball and threw it as hard as I could right at him. I think perhaps I expected to miss, but I did not. And when that snowball struck his face, he burst into noisy tears. His brother and his friends started yelling at me as he turned around to go back home. I walked away filled with shame. I knew I had done a bad thing. I learned that I could hurt another, which suddenly burdened me with greater responsibility for my actions. This is not a bad thing.

As children, we learned to be who we are by trial and error, and the errors were things we needed to help us grow. Still, I held onto all the feelings as well as the lessons, and as an adult, I found the feelings could paralyze my spirit.

Several years ago, I made a list of everything I could think of that produced that crippling, sinking feeling in my stomach—everything I held regrets about—going back all the way to kindergarten and before. Then I sat down with my list and my minister and went through item by item and told him what I was finished holding onto. He may have thought I was being too hard on myself, but there comes a time when we have to say, "The past is done. I am now." There comes a time when we have to start over and be able to lift our gazes from the airport floor, look into the eyes of a stranger and smile.

I've spent a lot of time working on issues. I know I have a lot more work to do. But I'm also sure I will never throw a snowball at your face. I've told you one of the tools I use to work this stuff out. I have to share one more. It is an easy one. It is a gem I found in a book of poems by a Milwaukee poet named Harvey Taylor. It is from his 1989 collection called "Torch Songs," which might still be available at Woodland Pattern Company. I've talked to him and told him that I make copies of this poem and hand it out all over. That pleases him, so I emailed him and asked if I could reproduce it for you in this book. He said, "Yes."

So here it is . . .

On the next page . . .

A Hot Tip

Harvey Taylor

It was one of those conversations
that range from here to the Himalayas:
children,
      seaweed,
    vacuum cleaners,
              donkeys,
      skyscrapers...

In the midst of it, she said,
    "Look, it's simple—
all your problems come from
being who you are,
so all you have to do
is be somebody else,
& they're gone.
But not just any
old somebody else,
'cause then you'd just be
carrying around their load—
no, someone new,
just born,
with each
      fresh
           breath..."

thanks, Deborah

I don't think I can improve upon that, so I will simply wish you joy and peace. And so it is.

TELLING TRUTH

Here's a nice little chestnut: The job of a minister is to comfort the afflicted and afflict the comfortable.

If ministers wanted only to say popular, feel-good things, we could become inspirational speakers and rev up the crowds at corporate annual meetings. But we're supposed to traffic in truth. Truth is sometimes unpopular.

Through the years I have belonged to many organizations that helped fulfill different needs in my life. Like most organizations, the ones I've been affiliated with like to refer to themselves as families, and in many ways, that is what they are. And like any family, every organization has a certain amount of dysfunctionality. Each one has skeletons in its closet. Each one has traditions that may not serve the highest good but are left unchallenged for reasons that are also not discussed.

The rules that govern taboo topics are simple:
1. Deny there is a problem.
2. If denial mechanisms break down, don't talk about what is really going on.

These rules help keep the peace. But it is a peace based upon lies. It is stagnant.

The qualities of Spirit include Truth and Life. Truth and Life are aspects of the same thing, so they are subject to the same laws. The law of life is growth; therefore, a law of truth is growth. When a lie is ignored, it becomes an institution that is not permitted to grow or to reveal a more profound—or at least more functional—version of itself.

Last week one of my friends was marveling at my ability to recall the details of my childhood. He asked whether my lessons evoke the memories or the memories evoke the lessons. I'm not sure I can answer that. The memories are always present, lurking around the periphery of my consciousness. They've been there since the incidents that formed them. The details haven't changed. But my interpretation of the details continues to change from year to year as the law of growth acts upon the truth to reveal more to me. If the memories were inaccurate—if I changed them to make them more palatable—their meanings could not change. I would simply make new lies to preserve the meaning of the old ones. I don't know if that's clear.

When I was in second grade, I got my first wristwatch. It was a little silver Timex with a black leather band. The inside of the band was unfinished bare leather. My mother took a laundry marker and carefully lettered my name on the inside of the band. This was important because kids tend to leave things lying around. Each morning when my class went to gym, those of us who wore watches would take them off and leave them lying on a steel serving counter that opened between the gym and the school kitchen. At the end of gym class, we would retrieve our watches—at least, that was the intent. One day about ten minutes after gym class, I realized I'd forgotten to pick up my watch. The teacher let me go back to the gym, but it wasn't there.

That year, a boy joined our class partway into the first term. His name was Roger. He was a little bit older than the rest of us, and a little bit bigger. His clothes were old. His pencils were chewed stubs without erasers. The only paper he had was the off-white stock with thick blue lines that the school provided for practicing penmanship—the kind that was so rough that it contained little chunks of wood where the pencil point would stick and tear a hole. Roger's family was clearly poor, and he no longer possessed the innocence that most second-graders enjoy.

After lunch on the day I lost my watch, I noticed Roger was wearing one that looked just like it. It stood out because it was the nicest thing he had. I asked him if he found it in the gym. He said, "No," and held up his arm for me to see, "My mother gave me that." I was sure he was lying. I knew if he took the watch off, we would see my name neatly printed inside the band. I could have asked the teacher to help. But it seemed easier to join the lie. Revealing the truth would have created uncomfortable tension, so the lie endured. I no longer owned a watch.

The next September, I was walking to school on a Monday morning with my neighborhood friends. The weather was still warm. The trees still had all their leaves. My friends were a year younger than me. They were in the same second-grade class as the youngest son of the minister of my church. To get to school, we had to walk past the church. On the ground next to the sidewalk, I spotted a watch. It looked just like the one I had lost the year before. I picked it up and strapped it on—considered it providence—and my friends and I all made a big deal about how fortunate I was.

When I got home that day, I showed my mother the watch, but I didn't tell her where I found it. I told her it was in the lost-and-found at school and must have spent the summer lying under a mitten. She accepted my word. But there was a significant difference between the watch I found and the one I lost. The one I found had a band that was polished black both inside and out. I took a Magic Marker and wrote my name on the metal back of the watch. I strapped it on and went out to play.

My friends met me at the edge of my yard. The minister's son from their class was with them. On Sunday evening, he had lost his watch. He had it in his shirt pocket after evening worship, but it must have fallen out when he was playing in the low branches of a maple tree next to the sidewalk. Everyone advised me to give him his watch back. But I was attached to the lie. I didn't want to give it up. I argued it was the watch I'd lost the year before—that my name was even written on the back. I took it off and showed them.

I don't remember the rest of the conversation except that I was all nerves and guilt. But somehow I came up with a rationalization for my keeping the watch, which began a drama of lies. The minister's wife called on the phone, and I listened to my mom tell my lost-and-found story. At that point, the lie became an institution. I repeated the lost-and-found story so often that I started believing it myself. I remember somehow being pushed into a conversation with the principal of the school and being told that the lost-and-found was cleaned out every summer. I had to ignore that inconvenient fact. It got very complicated. The two versions of how I found the watch must have crossed paths, but somehow, I ended up keeping it. I had to think of new stories to support the old lie, and everyone had to hear a different version that wouldn't conflict with the information they had. The whole situation was becoming unbearable for me. I told my mother I was going to return the watch, but she said I didn't have to. She chose to believe my first version of the story, and I couldn't bring myself to admit I'd lied to her.

My friends and the minister's son must have grown tired of the tension. They eventually dropped the topic altogether. I kept the watch out of my mind by leaving it in my underwear drawer instead of wearing it. The only person who wouldn't let it drop was the minister's oldest son. He was a year older than me. Whenever he saw me on the playground or around the neighborhood, he only said one thing to me: "Do you still have my brother's watch?"

Winter came and went. The air turned warm again. Summer vacation was approaching. The watch—my lie and the discomfort that went with it—still lay in my underwear drawer.

I stayed after school one day to finish a late assignment. I started walking home all alone. When I was in front of the church, the minister came out carrying a spiral notebook with green pages that were lined and divided into columns. He was friendly as always. He pointed at a page in the notebook and said, "I'm glad to see you. I just noticed that you've had perfect attendance at Sunday school. That means you can have half off the price of going to Bible camp. Why don't you talk it over with your parents? I'm sure you would really enjoy it."

That was the last straw for me. I knew the minister was lying. I did not have perfect attendance. I knew I missed at least three Sundays. And I could see he was lying in order to cure me of lying. He thought a week at Bible camp would make me re-think the whole business with the watch, but it did not need rethinking. I was exhausted from trying to keep the lie alive. Without telling my mother what I was going to do, I got the watch out of my underwear drawer and walked up to the parsonage. The first person I saw was the minister's youngest son. I held out his watch. "Here. This is yours." He was the happiest-looking boy that ever was. I was the happiest-feeling boy that ever was. And that was the end. Nobody ever brought it up again, and I remained friends with both of the minister's sons for years.

There was one hero in this long drama. It was the minister's oldest son. He wasn't willing to accept the lie. He wasn't willing to let it drop. He wasn't willing to try to trick me with new lies. He just clung relentlessly to the truth: "Do you still have my brother's watch?"

That incident did not cure me of lying. It just made me better at it. I learned to craft stories that couldn't be checked. I learned to keep only to a single version of each lie. But I also learned that a lie was always the end of the road. Once in place, it could not grow into something greater, whereas truth always grows greater. I could be a pretty good liar now. I've done enough research. But now I'm committed to growth.

Lies are tricky things. They can camouflage themselves among the truth. Some people might be offended when I tell the truth, but in the long run, I set them free. Sometimes I expose institutional lies that have gone unchallenged for years. Authority figures who are invested in the lies get angry. But I figure the sooner the lies fall apart, the better off everyone will be. Given that little bit of awareness, my new challenge to myself is to search my own consciousness for things I accept as facts but are really untrue. I have to observe the things I say to see if I give different versions to different people under different circumstances.

The thoughts that govern my inner world are like a family. They all must coexist in the same head. They all must share the same playground. Sometimes, they are going to disagree. I hope that most of the time they can live in harmony. The sneaky ones will try to craft new versions of reality for their own selfish benefit. The ones I have to really listen to are the relentless voices of Truth. They're always present. Sometimes I can hide from them, but I can't ignore them. They are qualities of Spirit, and they are all subject to the same immutable laws as Life, Love, Power, Peace, Beauty, Joy and Wisdom. They have the capacity to bring Light into the world. They are bound to teach me great things. And when they do, I'll let you know—because you are wonderful. And so it is.

JACK-O-LANTERN

It's a beautiful October evening, sweatshirt-warm, a little bit foggy, and very still. I was sitting on my porch, unwilling to come in and see what ideas would flow into the musings this week. It was such a peaceful night. And I was peaceful. And it felt like a blank page could best say what was on my mind. I began to wonder at how I have become whatever it is I am right now. In a given day, it seems I am so many things. Sometimes I'm a technician. Sometimes I am a minister. Sometimes I'm a writer. I am a student. I am a teacher. I am a friend. I am a loner. I am a housecleaner. I am a slob. I am smart. I am dopey. And it all swirls together and overlaps to make up this thing called my life.

As vague ideas about my life swirled and overlapped in the fog on my porch, the peaceful evening was invaded by the sound of a car alarm. The porch was suddenly no longer pleasant. Time to go inside. Time to be a writer.

24 hours ago, I was a pumpkin carver. I have a friend who is nine years old. She has never had a jack-o-lantern at Halloween. Her mother has never taken the time to try the pumpkin-carving craft. This year, they asked me for help. It was a tremendous gift. I like carving pumpkins, but it is not something I take time to do for myself. It's usually not a very high priority for me.

Through the years, the pumpkins I've carved have all looked basically the same. I've experimented with different types of eyes, but my noses have always been triangles. My mouths have always been wide grins with lots of pointed teeth.

This year was different. For one thing, it wasn't my pumpkin. This year, the pumpkin belonged to a little girl, and she chose a face from a picture in a pumpkin-carving instruction book. It was more intricate than any I've made before—with a crescent-shaped nose and extra cuts to form eyebrows and wrinkles at the corners of the eyes and mouth. It required a little more thought and attention than my previous carving projects.

My friend's pumpkin book warned us that the finished jack-o-lantern would not look exactly like the picture. It wisely pointed out that every pumpkin is different in size, shape and texture. To begin, all we had was an idea. Many factors would influence the final form.

First, we drew the face onto the pumpkin with a dry-erase marker, so we could wipe it off if we messed up. When our drawing looked pretty good, we cut open the top with a nice bevel, so it wouldn't fall through the opening when we put it back. I showed my friend how to clean the seeds and the slippery, stringy pulp from inside. She squealed and giggled a lot. She didn't know that creating a jack-o-lantern would be so slimy and messy. My friend's mom got a little agitated at the noise. I had to point out that squealing and giggling were part of the process. It was a pumpkin party. It's gross. That's half the fun.

When the inside of the pumpkin was scraped clean, we started carving the face using a kid-safe pumpkin saw. I had never used one before. It really did work much better than a steak knife. Since it was my friend's first pumpkin, we took turns. I demonstrated the tricks of the craft, and then she would try. When I saw her do something the hard way, or when I saw her do something that might cause a problem with the design—like cutting off a tooth or carving outside the lines—I would caution her. When I did, she would apologize. I found that peculiar. The third time she said, "I'm sorry," I explained that I was not scolding her. I told her I was teaching her. It was her first pumpkin. I didn't expect her to know how to do it. I had to remind her that we were having fun.

When the jack-o-lantern was finished, we lit a candle, put it inside, and turned out the lights. It was very cool. It looked scary and funny at the same time. It was an ugly face, but lighted from within, it was a thing of beauty—a thing of nature shaped to be a work of art. It felt almost as if we had created a life.

As I ponder tonight over the life I've created for myself, I can see parallels to carving a pumpkin. I began with an idea. I opened the top and dug out all the slimy stuff. I whittled and carved according to the factors dictated by size, shape and texture. And now, it isn't exactly what I had in mind.

When I look at the process, I wonder how it might have been different. Could it have been more fun? How often have I been agitated by squeals and giggles? Probably many times. I have to remember that sometimes they are appropriate. Even though this carving of a life is a creative process, it's also a party. It's okay squeal and giggle. It's supposed to be fun.

I wonder, too, how often have I felt I needed to apologize for not knowing something? How many times have I avoided learning because I was afraid to have someone correct me? Undoubtedly, many times. I have to remember that life is going to include lessons. I learn them from other people. When they offer me advice, they are not scolding me. They teach me because they love me.

The jack-o-lantern I helped carve last night was not my first. I've carved at least a dozen. And I made some errors that drastically affected how they turned out. I've forgotten to bevel the top and had to prop it up with toothpicks. I've used a too-sharp steak knife and sliced eyeholes all the way into the nose. I've lopped off teeth. But there are always more pumpkins. And every one I've carved was better than the last.

Just as there are always more pumpkins, I have a lot more life. From the carving I've done so far, I've learned some tools and techniques that work very well. As time goes by I will learn other things that work even better. But the most important thing for me to remember is that no matter how many mistakes I made in the carving, all of the pumpkins I carved looked good with a lighted candle inside. This thing that is my life can sometimes look funny. It can sometimes look ugly or scary. But when my inner light shines, it's a thing of beauty. And so it is.

GRATITUDE

It is my opinion that Thanksgiving is the purest of holidays, and it offers the opportunity for the most wonderful spiritual practice.

The reason I call it a "pure" holiday is that unlike all the others, it requires no patriotic or dogmatic affiliation. It isn't a holiday that implies, "We are celebrating the fact that we are the chosen ones." It is simply a time to enjoy family or friends and to thank the Giving Universe for all that we have and hold dear. It is a holiday when veterans can sit down with conscientious objectors. Christians can sit down with Atheists. Jews can sit with Muslims. Even Democrats and Republicans can observe it together (but be careful what you talk about). Nobody can say, "This is our holiday. You have no right to observe it." It is just a time to be grateful.

The reason it is wonderful spiritual practice is simply because it's easy. It is effective. What more could we ask for? If you're not used to hearing spiritual practice qualified by degree of difficulty, I'll give you an example. Tonight I went to the little room I call my chapel to practice meditation. By definition, meditation should be easy. It means to simply sit still, relax, do nothing and think about nothing. When I was in high school, I did that seven hours a day.

You'd think I'd have mastered it. But tonight, it was difficult.

First of all, I had trouble giving it time. My thinking was that if I spent a half hour in meditation, that would be a half hour later I would start writing and a half hour later that I would get to bed. There was a flaw in this train of thought. When I do not meditate, I write slowly because there is too much monkey chatter going on in my head. I know this well. Yet, as I tried to get settled upon my cushion, the monkeys were winning. Then in my agitated state, the candles I had burning were flickering just enough to distract me. My wandering attention then noticed the city sounds outside. And each of those sounds triggered a memory. Each memory tried to demand to be written down. I struggled for a half hour and calmed my mind for about a minute.

Now compare that spiritual practice to gratitude. I have a friend who taught me a trick. She is a spiritual genius. One Friday night several years ago, she was driving home from dinner at a restaurant with friends. The evening had been pleasant. Her life was in good order. Everything was fine. But for no apparent reason, she was overcome with anger. Perhaps it was a conditioned response to being on the highway. But it doesn't matter what triggered it. She was angry for no reason, and she didn't like it. So she reeled in her mind and started making a mental list of all the things she had to be grateful for. Within minutes, the anger was gone. It was replaced with a sense of peace and fulfillment.

That was a turning point in her spiritual awareness. She had found a perfect tool for achieving inner peace. That was years ago. To this day, she still keeps a gratitude journal. She writes in it a lot. She has filled several notebooks. It always produces the same effect. She always achieves a sense of peace and fulfillment. We all can do the same thing. Most people don't.

My inner cynic believes that most Americans are gratitude challenged. We live in a culture that encourages consumption by continually reminding us of what we don't have. People focus outwardly on products (or people) that they think will bring them happiness.

Zen Buddhism teaches that all human suffering comes from unfulfilled desires. When we look for things that are missing from our lives, we create suffering. To relieve our suffering, we can desire what we already have by appreciating what we already have. We do it through gratitude.

I don't mean to give desire a bad rap. It is certainly a part of us. If the Universe didn't want to fulfill our desires, we wouldn't be able to have them in the first place. But whatever we place our attention upon grows in our experience. When we are focused upon desire, the thing that grows is the desire, not the object of the desire. So when desire arises, we can bless it and turn attention back to gratitude. Don't worry about holding onto the desire. God didn't miss it. Nothing escapes the attention of the Universe. By focusing upon what we have, we are inviting God to give us more because It loves receiving our thanks.

I've borrowed the spiritual practice of listing my gratitude from my friend. I'm not as disciplined as she is. I do not keep a journal. But I frequently make mental lists of all I have to be grateful for. I always find new things to add to it. I like to focus on details—things I tend to take for granted. I just ate some yogurt. Rather than be disappointed that I didn't have ice cream, I chose to be grateful for my spoon. Can you imagine eating yogurt with chopsticks? When I drive, I am grateful for pavement, and brake lights, windshields, windshield wipers and the radio. There are many wonderful things that make driving safe and pleasant. I want to appreciate them all.

I am grateful for electricity. I'm grateful for my TV, and I'm grateful I can turn it off any time I want. I'm grateful for hot water, soap, coffee, toothpaste, refrigeration, pencils, erasers, paper and bananas. There are many things I enjoy everyday. They are all gifts from God. I want to keep them coming. So I'm grateful.

I invite you to join me in gratitude. It's Thanksgiving. You were going there anyway, but try to take it to a deeper level. If you're doing the cooking, remember to be grateful for your hot pads. If you're doing the eating, be grateful for the elasticity of your stomach. If you're overwhelmed by it all, try meditation, but when the monkeys start their chatter, remember you have a tool to drown them out. And so it is.

LOVING A TRAIN WRECK

I have a new houseguest. She moved in last night. She's cute, in her own little way. I don't know her name. And I don't think she likes me. She won't let me touch her. But she's quiet, and she uses the litter box the way she should.

A few nights ago a friend called me to say she had rescued a cat from a dangerous life outside in a bad neighborhood. My friend went on about how adorable this cat was. She described her as having long, tortoise-shell fur and a sweet disposition. Of course, living outside, she had a few challenges. Her beautiful long coat was full of burrs. She was grossly malnourished. And she was pretty badly beaten up with patches of fur pulled out and an eye missing. But she was cute in her own little way.

My friend took her to the vet on Friday morning and learned she had fleas and worms and she might be pregnant. She just keeps getting cuter, doesn't she? Fortunately for this nameless little thing, my friend could see beyond appearances and paid the vet to patch her up and treat all her undesirable conditions. It turned out that she wasn't pregnant, and now because of my friend's generosity, she never will be. By the time I was introduced to her, the wounds had been tended, infections treated, and the burrs had been shaved from her tail. My first impression was that she looked like a train wreck. But she's cute in her own little way.

Then after all of my friend's good deeds, her landlady told her to get that beast out of the house immediately if not sooner. So I have a new houseguest. I already have two cats—a gentle, shy one and a big brute of a thing who plays way too rough. These are adult cats. The gentle one is 10 years old. The brute is 7. Enter the train wreck. Judging by her size, she's probably less than a year old. She's tiny. But she's had a hard life, and she growls at the rest of us. Being safe is new to her. She hasn't figured out what it means.

So tonight, I'm trying to figure out how to teach love to a growling little train wreck. I tried speaking her language. I crawled around on the floor meowing. I sang her the song from the Meow Mix commercial.

I trailed a piece of ribbon around, so she could chase it. I gave her treats. And although she will eat Whisker Lickins out of my hand (mainly because she's half starved), she won't let me pet her. The only thing I can do is to let her be who she is. The love is present, but she has to find it within herself. I know it's there. When I was on the floor near her, I gazed into her eye, and saw the sweetness of her soul gazing back at me—even as she growled a warning to stay away (unless I had more treats).

A few years ago, a friend of mine had to have his cat put to sleep. His heart was broken, and he asked me if I thought animals had souls. He had been raised in a religious tradition that said only humans have souls. My response was simple. Of course animals have souls. That is how we grow to love them. Love is the affinity of souls to each other.

The souls find bodies and isolate themselves in the bodies in order to have the joyous experience of seeking each other out and reconnecting. When our pets or our friends or our families are finished with the in-body experience, when they go on to the next plane of experience, our hearts break, and we grieve because the soul connections, as we've learned to know them, are lost. I know people who say they love their cars or their shoes or mint chocolate chip ice cream, but that is a misuse of the word. We can have strong preferences for all the various consumer goods that people claim to love, but we can't really love without a soul connection. We might be disappointed, but our hearts don't break when our cars wear out or the ice cream is gone.

Tonight, I know this little nameless entity with one eye and a shaved tail has a soul. And I believe my soul and her soul found each other for a reason. I will be patient with her. I will honor her space. I will gaze into her eye, and I will cherish her soul. I can't make her love me. But I can love her, and I will do so willingly without thought of reward. And maybe, if I can get really good at it, I can extend this same courtesy to humans. Maybe I can practice loving without thought of reward upon all of the people in my life. Maybe I will let them be who they are and honor their souls as I know in my heart that we found each other for a reason and it wasn't to judge or shape or be annoyed with each other.

And maybe I'm looking at my relationship to the train wreck backwards. Maybe it isn't my job to teach her to love at all. Maybe it is what she is here to teach me. After all, I'm the one sitting here judging. I'm the one listing her ailments as if it is my job to decide what perfection does and does not look like. She is what she is. Apparently she is good enough for God. And as she fills her place in the Universe, perhaps she is the essence of perfection. Certainly, perfection is at her essence.

Tonight, I will let this new, one-eyed houseguest be my guide as I enter into the holiday season. A few years ago, I received a Christmas card that read "Love is the Reason for the Season." There must be some power in that statement. I normally don't memorize Christmas cards as I receive them. But I do remember Love is the Reason for the Season. So tonight I will let the holiday season begin. I will welcome it by recognizing its essence. I will honor the season by consciously loving. I will begin at home by loving my house full of cats. I will extend that feeling out to the entire world. And of course, that includes you—because you are wonderful. And so it is.

DOT-TO-DOT

When I was a little boy, I loved drawing the little number puzzles called dot-to-dots. I thought it was terrific fun. I would put my pencil on point number one, move it to point two, on to three, four, five . . . When I got up to about 63 or so, a picture would emerge. It might be a rhinoceros, or a Christmas tree, or a house. I think I was supposed to color them when the dots were all connected, but I never did. The pictures were not good enough to bother coloring. I just liked connecting the dots to see what would emerge.

****

This year is the first year in my adult life that I decorated the outside of my house with Christmas lights. It has always seemed like a bother. Christmas comes when the weather is cold. Putting up lights involves standing on a ladder with the cold December wind blowing up my trousers. What's worse, taking the lights down requires climbing the same ladder in January when the wind is even colder. I don't know about you, but if I wanted to work outside in cold weather, I would have been a cowboy. When the weather gets cold, I like to turn up the heat and snuggle in with a book. But this year, I decorated.

I didn't get carried away like some of my neighbors. I kept it very simple. I wanted to put up a symbol of what the season means to me, so I cut a peace sign from a piece of plywood, drilled 200 holes around the edges of the sign, inserted the blue bulbs from two strings of lights in the holes, and hung the assembly on my front porch. Making the peace sign took a little work, but hanging it was quick and easy. Taking it down will be easier still.

On the lawn—just below the peace sign—is a pile of rubble. My house just got a new roof, and the roofers dumped the scraps of trimmed shingles and packaging materials in a pile in front of the porch. I trust they will be back in the morning to clean up, but for now the peace sign over the pile of rubble makes a poignant image in light of the things that go on in the world.

****

In New Thought, we teach that everything begins with an idea. Our lives are like a movie of what is going on in our minds. All our beliefs—the conscious ones as well as repressed and forgotten ones—shape our experiences. As one of my teachers says, if you want to see the state of your mind, look at your house. This is comforting to me when my house is clean and orderly. It kind of pisses me off when the house is a mess. When every horizontal surface is covered in dust and clutter, I know I have two messes to clean up—one within and one without.

I have one room in my house that always stays clean. It is dedicated to meditation. It is lightly furnished with a small, simple altar, a few sacred symbols from my favorite religions, a little bookstand/reading table, and a meditation cushion. It is the place I sit to meditate. I guess you already figured that out. The point is that it always stays clean, which suggests that if I could stay in meditation as I go about my daily business, my whole house would stay clean, not to mention my truck and my desk at work.

****

I first heard of meditation about the same time I learned about the peace sign. It's funny that I embrace them both with all my heart. When I was first exposed to them, I was taught they were sinful. I was a teenager. It was in the sixties, and America was torn in debate over our involvement in Vietnam. The church I belonged to was very conservative. It stood behind the war effort and rejected any questioning of authority. I was taught that meditation was a mystical, occult practice that would lead me away from God, and I was told that the peace sign was a satanic symbol of a broken cross. Even in my adolescent mind, I sensed there was something really wrong with that. I could see where someone might spot a broken cross in a peace sign, but I also saw that the proportions were all wrong. I recognized too that a symbol is as good as the meaning one associates with it. I saw millions of Americans holding up a symbol for peace, and I saw none of them worshipping a devil. I tried digging around in my Bible for an answer about meditation, and just like promoting peace, meditation really seemed like something Jesus would do.

I began looking at my religion critically, and some serious flaws emerged. It seemed to be built upon impossible assumptions that were never questioned or even acknowledged as being questionable. The whole structure presupposed a God that would condemn and destroy Its own creation. That seemed unlikely. There was also the issue of a book. We had a book that was regarded as flawless. But I was taught that the only thing that was flawless was God. But God wasn't the book. So it seemed that the book was a false God. I told that to my Sunday school teacher. I think he saw it coming because he didn't miss a beat as he blurted out a response that seemed rehearsed. With absolute authority, he misquoted Romans 13.1—completely out of context—and twisted it around to mean that I was supposed to kowtow to higher authority, and that higher authority was to be found in him and in the church and in the government. I nodded to indicate I understood, and I quit the church to become a hippie. Yippee.

****

The room in which I meditate has a single heat register, but it does not have a cold-air-return duct. When the door is closed, air can't circulate. The door is closed all the time to keep the cats out. This time of year, it gets pretty chilly. Sitting in meditation can be a little uncomfortable, but I've discovered that I can keep myself warm by simply placing two burning candles on the floor—one on either side of me. Just two tiny flames produce enough heat to keep the chill away.

As I look at my peace sign with a critical eye, I think of how similar it is to the candles. The flames from my candles radiate heat. The message on my porch radiates peace. Just as the flames from the candles alter the environment in my meditation room, the light of peace on my front porch alters the environment of the world. It may not be much, but it is something.

****

When I was a little boy, I loved solving dot-to-dots, but only if they were good ones. Sometimes, I would find one in a newspaper or a magazine, and its creator would have drawn in the detail. The dots only connected the basic outline. I could see at a glance—without even touching the paper—what the picture was going to be. That took all the fun out of it. It was kind of insulting, and the mystery of the creative process was lost.

****

The past few months have been turbulent for me. I've been catching myself entertaining desires for things to be different. I've been angry. I've been lonely. I've been stressed. For these things to change, my thoughts must change first, so I've been working to realign my mind and my heart with the way I want my life to look. I've been redirecting my focus to entertain only quiet thoughts of peace. So far, I've been fairly successful at quieting my heart. My mind has not yet caught up. I'm still connecting the dots.

Among the noises in my head are my thoughts about my peace sign. I've observed myself worrying that I might have offended the people across the street. They responded to the peace sign by putting an American flag smack in the middle of their holiday display. And I hear myself thinking that if the neighbors don't like it, what about the people driving past? And then I catch myself wondering if it does any good at all. In this troubled world, can one blue peace sign affect any sort of change? Yet in the silence of my heart, I know it makes a difference. In the silence of my heart, I know I make a difference. In the silence of my heart, I know you make a difference. In the silence of my heart, I know that you are wonderful. And so it is.

THE WALL

I'm struggling to break down a wall around my heart. It's a funny wall. It allows love to flow out, but it keeps it from flowing in. It's like one of those two-way mirrors in the department store that allows security personnel to see out while others cannot see in. I'm sitting on the security side. It gets lonely in here.

I wasn't even aware of the wall until recently. As I said, it allows love to flow out. I'm sure security guards behind two-way mirrors in stores take a little time to adjust. Being able to see out, I imagine, at first it must feel as if people can also see in. But eventually, they realize that nobody can see in. Then they can do their jobs without feeling self-conscious. But suppose they were placed behind the mirror, yet they believed it was a regular window. They would sit and look out at others. They could smile and wave. They would have a hard time understanding why people didn't respond the way they expected. In many ways, that's what's been happening with this wall on my heart. And it's been happening for a long, long time.

Of course, I cannot speak in absolutes. Sometimes, and with some people, the wall has portals that open up. But I've learned that all too frequently, the portals slam shut. It ain't supposed to be that way. But as I said, I didn't know it was happening. Now I know. Now the work begins. But I don't know where to start. I've asked a few friends for their ideas. I've gained a few helpful insights. And I guess that's what I need right now—a little help, a little communication.

Last night as I was pondering this problem, I thought about the fact that I don't cry much. Sometimes, this concerns me. I had to think back about what makes me cry. It seemed like a good place to look for clues—a good way to better understand the wall. I had to think back a long, long time.

I remembered watching "Mister Magoo's Christmas Carol" as a boy. I watched it every year. I haven't seen it for years, but in my memory, it really was a masterpiece. It appealed to children, yet it contained all of the important elements of the original Dickens classic. And it made me cry. It made me laugh too. It was supposed to do that I guess. But the part that made me cry every year-the part that can still make me cry as I think about it now—was when young Ebenezer Scrooge was left at boarding school for the holidays. The Ghost of Christmas Past took Mister Magoo back to that place and time, and young Ebenezer sang "I'm All Alone in the World." Mister Magoo, the grown-up Ebenezer, stood behind his child self and sang along. It was deeply touching to me. I remember shielding my face, so my sister and my parents would not see my tears. After all, it was only a cartoon, and boys weren't supposed to cry. But somehow, I felt like young Scrooge. Last year at Christmas, I felt like old Scrooge. Could this wall around my heart have been here all these years? Evidence says yes. This is frightening to me.

I'm exploring new territory. I like having all the right answers. Right now, I'm having trouble formulating the right questions. But there is a Universal Spirit that is always speaking. It knows what I do not. I'm sure there have been times in my life when the wall was down—or when the portals were open. That seems to be a likely place to start searching.

Several years ago, the cellular phone company that I work for had a Thanksgiving outreach program. Employees volunteered to go to homeless shelters and soup kitchens on Thanksgiving Day. We went equipped with banks of cellular phones, and we let the patrons make phone calls. They could call whomever they wanted. The thought behind it was that most of the homeless people had friends or family, here or in another city, and if they could reconnect, it would ease the loneliness of being homeless. Perhaps they could connect with someone who would help them. It sounded like a worthwhile bit of charity, so I signed up for the breakfast shift at a downtown church. My portals were opened that day.

When I went to the church in the morning, I went with trepidation. I was afraid of homeless people. I thought they would regard me with suspicion and contempt. At the same time, I knew I needed the experience. I wanted to offer the gift of myself. So I showed up at the church and gathered with my co-workers to offer our services. Our group was large. We had more people than we had phones. Staffing the tables was a little bit awkward.

Some of the people in the group had done this the year before. They took charge of the phone equipment. That left a few of us first-timers to be greeters. We were to guide the homeless into orderly lines. The judgments that I arrived with made the task seem intimidating. I had a fear that the people we were dealing with did not value order. We finished setting up our tables and staffing our positions at the same time the kitchen volunteers were ready to begin serving breakfast. The doors to the church basement were unlocked. I expected a disorderly stampede to the food and the phones. I was completely wrong.

People began to trickle in. They were quiet and respectful. The men removed their hats as they came through the door. Some let the ladies ahead of them in line. They filed through the food line then gathered at the dining tables in small groups to eat their breakfasts. As they sat talking amongst each other, it looked like any cafeteria. Their table manners and the things they talked about were the same as in the lunchroom at work. After they had eaten and bused their tables, they started forming lines to use the phones. They did not need to be herded. They were regular adults with regular manners. Their clothes were old and torn. Many of them were missing teeth. They looked tired and drawn. But their souls were intact, and they responded to the opportunity to reach out to loved ones with gratitude and grace.

My teacher that day was one of the women from my office. She was assigned to greeting with me. At work, she was a manager, and that morning, she was dressed very nicely. By her clothing, she really looked out of place. But she seemed to have arrived with no preconceptions. When she looked at the people standing in line, she did not see homeless people. She just saw people, and she wanted to meet them. She opened her heart and started asking their names. She walked up and down the line and found out where people came from, whom they were planning to call, and where they were planning to go later. She learned where Thanksgiving dinners were being offered that afternoon, and she made sure everybody knew. She did all this with absolute respect. She was not condescending. She honestly made friends, and people started telling her about themselves. They told her their plans—things like where they were going to look for work and how they intended to get back on their feet.

I tried to emulate her. I tried to engage the people they way that she did. But I couldn't quite pull it off. I asked the same kinds of questions. I gave the same kinds of reassurances. But she was connected. I was just going through the motions.

It was the heart thing. My heart was open to giving, but I didn't want to accept anything back. My heart was closed to anything the people had to offer. But my friend—the manager—had her heart open wide. What flowed out was allowed to flow back in. One of the men in the line who had spoken to her said to me, "That sure is a classy lady," and he was sincere. She knew how to give and receive love, and people recognized and appreciated it.

Even though I couldn't connect with the people as well as my manager friend, the experience changed me. I remember it well. That holiday season was a good one for me. I enjoyed the decorations. I enjoyed the music. I enjoyed the shopping and the parties and the family gatherings. It was an open-heart season. But it seems that in the past few years, the portals that were opened have been silently—almost imperceptibly—closing up. I'm grateful to be aware of it, but I really have my work cut out for me. I don't want to have another Mister Magoo Christmas. I want to experience the best that the season has to offer, and I know it is all up to me.

Christmas season doesn't change much from year to year. I do. So tonight, I'm declaring the official start of my holiday season. I'm going to enjoy it even if it means putting up a tree. I'm going to enjoy it even if it means listening to Kenny G playing "Have Yourself A Merry Little Christmas."

I have much to be grateful for. I have loving friends who want to help me tear down the wall around my heart. I have good memories that help me see ways in which I can do it. So this is the year the wall comes down for good, and if you have a wall of your own, I invite you to bring yours down as well—-because you are wonderful. And so it is.

AUTUMN BLIZZARD

Only ten more days until winter! That means that right now in Wisconsin, we are having an autumn blizzard. This is good. It means springtime can come in January.

I know that some of you live in warmer places. Well, I don't want to sound like I'm bragging, but here in Milwaukee, we have nine inches of fluffy white, and it's still falling. It is extreme. It is exciting. This is abundant life.

When I got home from work, I surveyed the abundance and thought I should probably start shoveling. Naturally, I went straight upstairs and took a nap.

You can't rush into these things. As I was napping, I had a dream. In the dream there was a blizzard, which I responded to by taking a nap. When I awoke from the nap (the one in the dream), the snow had stopped falling. The sun was shining, and all the snow was melting away from the sidewalks.

That is usually the way it is around here. It snows. It melts. When it is falling, it feels like it will never stop. It seems like we will be buried. Then the sun comes out, and it feels like, "Gee, that was nothing; it didn't even set a record." And life goes back to being pretty much the way it always is—without the extremes to make it exciting. It's interesting to note how life imitates itself everywhere. One day I'm buried in blowing and drifting work, phone calls, pain or pleasure. The next day, everything is calm, and it all melts away.

I frequently use a warm-weather, coastal metaphor when people ask me about my life – especially when things do not appear to be going well. If I'm having a day when I'm feeling lonely, somebody will invariably ask me, "How's your love life?"

I'm keenly aware of the power of the spoken word. I know everything I say is a prayer. I certainly don't want to affirm the loneliness by talking about it. At the same time, I can't tell lies. So they ask, "How's your love life." And I answer, "The tide comes in; the tide goes out." They usually chuckle a little, then they scurry off before I say something even stranger. But the truth remains. The tide comes in; the tide goes out.

When I awoke from my nap (the real one), the snow was still falling. The sun was not out. The roads and sidewalks were not clear. I was out of excuses, so I put on my snow pants and boots. I wore my heavy coat, my fuzzy hat and my insulated gloves, and I went outside to work. It's 14 degrees (Fahrenheit) outside (-7 C). Within minutes, I was roasting. I had to come back inside and change into a lighter jacket and hat. I switched from insulated to fingerless gloves. 14F is a good shoveling temperature. It keeps the snow light and fluffy. It keeps me from getting too warm. Things are never as bad as they seem.

Shoveling can be pleasant work. It doesn't require any thought. As I worked, I sang a Kate Wolf's song, "Give Yourself to Love" over and over. I hummed my way through the words I couldn't remember. Every so often, a big gust of wind would send clouds of snow swirling around me, so I would stop shoveling, squint to keep it out of my eyes, hold my breath and enjoy the cool, wet particles that found their way down my back. Sooner than I expected, the shoveling was finished.

Keeping with an old family tradition, I came inside and made hot chocolate. But I wasn't cold. I didn't need warming up. I sat in my underwear trying to cool off as I drank it. Traditions are stupid. I could have had ice water. Maybe there is a good reason people scurry away from me when I tell them, "The tide comes in; the tide goes out."

Looking out the window, I see it is time to shovel again. This time, I will dress a little more lightly. Maybe I'll sing a different song. Maybe I will drink cold water when I'm finished. It doesn't matter. It's all good. God is still doing what God always does—creating in abundance, giving me more than I need of everything.

Today I will remember that snow is a gift. As I know that everything in the Universe is part of the Infinite One, I am reminded that snow holds moisture in the soil to condition the fields to grow the bounty of food upon my table. As I eat in my warm kitchen, I am grateful for the snow. As I look out upon the snow, I am grateful that I am not hungry. As I commune with my friend, the snow, by shoveling it from my drive and walkways, my heart and muscles vibrate with gratitude for the invigorating exercise the snow has imposed upon my daily routine. I am grateful to have my routine interrupted, as I know that unscheduled activities stimulate new thoughts and feelings. When I am in my home, I am grateful to the snow for giving me a good reason to stay indoors with a good book. As I drive in the snow, I am grateful for the opportunity to drive a little bit slower, to hear a few more songs on the radio, to look upon the beauty of it and admire God's handiwork. I am grateful for the opportunity to connect at a soul level with my fellow drivers as we are all forced to drive more mindfully, to cooperate with each other more consciously and to regard each other's safety more carefully. We are all part of the Infinite One, and any sense of inconvenience I might blame upon the snow is displaced by a positive, loving sense of gratitude for all the gifts it brings to my life. And so it is.

HONG KONG CHRISTMAS

We're on the home stretch, and it appears I'm going to make it. I've spent a lot of years being Christmas-challenged, but I think that I'm going to get through this one in comfort and joy. Perhaps I'm enjoying the season because I decided I would. Decision is powerful stuff. Or perhaps I'm just growing up. A spiritually mature person is comfortable with opposites and recognizes all the good things nestled all snug among the bad. Everything that exists is the product of a confluence of factors and forces. I'm having a good Christmas season for a bunch of reasons, but it's mainly because I choose to. That's really all it takes.

In 1977, I spent Christmas in Hong Kong Harbor. I was in the Navy. I was far from my home, far from my family, and I'd resigned myself to having no Christmas at all that year. Then came an announcement. As a goodwill gesture, the ship had arranged to host a Christmas party for a group of orphans. Interested crew members were invited to help out. There weren't many. Most of the crew had taken the water taxi to drink themselves silly on shore. All that remained aboard were those of us who were on duty.

My first thought was that a warship was an inappropriate place to entertain children. But I didn't see how boycotting the party was going to improve anything. I decided that for a few hours, I would celebrate Christmas. I even decided to enjoy it. So I was on hand when the children arrived.

About thirty kids were ferried out just after the noon meal. The mess deck was decorated with balloons and crepe paper. It looked more like a birthday party than Christmas. We fed the children hotdogs and chips, which they ate. They were all quiet and polite—thoroughly unchildlike. Cake and ice cream perked them up a little. They started talking and laughing among themselves. But they were leery of the sailors who shuffled around in a few little awkward groups wondering what we were supposed to be doing.

The children stayed in their chairs, which they had pushed together into little clumps, so they could huddle and hold onto each other. They looked around with wide eyes and looks on their faces that seemed to say, "What are they going to do to us?" I felt bad. I felt helpless. I felt we were failing our mission. Then came Santa.

One of our Chief Petty Officers (a fat one) came out in full uniform. He had the red suit and black boots. He wore a long white beard, and he had a large sack slung over his shoulder. I wondered at first if the significance of the character might be lost because of cultural differences. But the children all smiled. They weren't too keen on sailors, but they knew who Santa Claus was.

The children took turns sitting on Santa's lap. Each one got a gift from Santa's sack. Toys to play with melted the ice—put us sailors into navigable waters. We weren't sure how to talk to the children, but we did know how to play. That's when we learned that most of the children spoke English. We talked about Christmas. The children spoke more about Jesus than about Santa Claus. The sailors mostly spoke wistfully about home.

The party was going well, except I noticed two little girls who were sitting apart from the group clinging to one another. One looked very sad. Her companion was whispering to her in Chinese. I sat down near them and said hello. I tried to put on a let's-be-friends smile.

The girl who was talking could see I wanted to help, so she told me the problem. "This is first Christmas without her mommy and father. She does not speak English, so she feels bad here."

I don't speak Chinese. I was 22 years old, and wasn't sure how to talk to kids. But both girls looked at me like I ought to do something, so I pulled my harmonica from my pocket and raised it to my mouth. The sad girl's eyes opened wide, and she almost smiled. I started improvising a sort of blues/boogie tune. The girl cocked her head to one side and wrinkled her forehead. That music didn't do it for her. So I tried playing "Gloria In Excelsis Deo." That hit the spot. She showed me a big picket-fence grin. She was losing her baby teeth.

The girl who spoke English said, "Yes. Yes. Keep playing more." She gave her friend a big squeeze. I played "Silent night." The little gap-toothed girl whispered something to her friend who said, "She would like to play a song for you too."

I handed my harmonica to my new friend, and she played a medley of Stephen Foster tunes. As she tooted through "Old Suzanna" and "Old Folks At Home," the rest of the children were gathering for a tour of the ship. I didn't want to make her stop playing, so I picked her up and followed the tour group. The harmonica player's friend—our interpreter—stayed at my side; although, her services were no longer needed. I carried the little musician in my right arm. She'd play for a while, and then she'd push the harmonica up to my mouth. I'd take hold of it with my left hand and play something, then I would hand it back and she would play some more.

The three of us never fully connected with the rest of the group. Most of the children took turns sitting in the ship's helicopter and mounting the seats of the three-inch guns. My two friends and I stayed near the rails and looked out over the acres of boats, many of which served as homes. We didn't talk much, but it didn't feel like we needed to.

At the end of the afternoon, the ferry came to take the children back to the orphanage. They filed down the accommodation ladder. I played "The Little Drummer Boy" for my two friends until they were the only ones left on deck. When it was their turn, my girls stepped down to the platform at the top of the ladder clutching the red plastic helicopters that Santa had given them. They turned back to look at me. The English-speaking girl and I said goodbye. I looked at the harmonica player. She looked unhappy again. I held out my harmonica to her. She just looked at me. I said, "Tell her to take it. It's hers."

The girls said a few words back and forth. Smiling her picket-fence smile, my friend reached up and took the harmonica from my hand and said something in Chinese.

"She say, 'Thank you.'"

"Merry Christmas."

"Merry Christmas."

I watched the ferry pull away. Most of the children sat in the hold to stay warm. My friends stood at the stern of the upper deck. The interpreter stood waving. The other sent soft music across the vast expanse of the harbor. My shipmates went below deck. I stood at the rail until the passengers on the ferry were no longer distinguishable.

I didn't feel loneliness at spending Christmas so far from home. I didn't feel I'd missed anything. I felt a little sadness for the two friends I'd never see again. But mostly I felt comfort and joy. There are good reasons for that. You know what they are. And so it is.

PULLING THE GOAT

When I was a boy, I occasionally went horse-back riding at Glengary Stables with my friends. Sometimes I went with neighborhood friends. Sometimes I went with the youth group from church. When I went with the youth group, I didn't arrange to ride with one of the carloads being driven by one of the stay-at-home moms. Instead, I would ride my bicycle to the stable and meet up with everyone there. It was several miles south of town, but I had a thing about taking care of myself. I didn't want to be beholdin' to nobody. I was the lonesome cowboy on a Sears 3-speed. Yee-haw!

In case the wind was against me, I gave myself plenty of lead-time to ride to the stable. That meant I usually got there first. On one trip when I was about 14, I got to the stable, and the parking lot was empty. The stable was at the back of the parking lot. On the side of the lot near the road was a house. Between the house and the parking lot, I saw two grimy little boys wrestling with a goat. The boys were nine or ten years old. The goat was a little bit bigger than an Irish setter.

The goat was their pet, and it had gotten out of its pen. Their mother was hanging laundry on the clothesline, and she was yelling at the boys to put the goat away, which is what they were trying to do. They were pulling on its horns, trying to lead it, but the harder they pulled, the harder the goat pulled. The goat was stronger than the boys. They kept falling down in the dust. The goat seemed to be laughing at them. It looked like tremendous fun, but the boys were getting frustrated.

When it was clear that the goat was going to win, the boys told their mother they were going to get a rope. She just shook her head and kept hanging laundry. The boys ran across the parking lot toward the stable. The goat watched them go.

When the mother picked up her empty laundry basket and went into the house, I saw an opportunity. I'd never played with a goat before, but I had been observing closely. I thought I could outwit it. I saw how the goat had resisted all the boys' tugs, and I suspected they were going about it all wrong. So with nobody watching, I walked over to the goat, and gently placed the palm of my hand against his forehead, right in front of his horns.

The goat immediately pushed against my hand. When I pulled my hand away, the goat stopped pushing. I put my hand back, and he pushed again. I left my hand in place, and the goat advanced. I kept enough pressure on him to keep him interested, and I slowly started walking backwards. The goat kept walking forward, trying to push harder against my hand. When I moved my hand to the right side of the goat's head, he turned to the right. When I moved my hand to the left, he turned to the left. When I saw how easy he was to steer, I simply and gently guided him into his pen. Then I closed the gate and latched it.

Before the boys got back with the rope, cars carrying my friends began to arrive. I tried to brag about my goat-handling expertise. But we were kids, and my friends didn't give a goat's ass about any goats. So we just went about the kid business of having a good time and trying to act cool. Now, years later, the goat is among my spiritual teachers. He taught me a better way of confronting problems.

Recently, I decided to tear down a wall around my heart. That is what I'm doing. But I'm not doing it with force. I'm doing it with a gentle touch. I'm maintaining enough pressure against the problem to remain engaged, but I'm not tugging and fighting and letting it drag me through the dirt.

I am a perfect channel of the Love of God—and so are you. And so it is.

PLAYING IN DARKNESS

Are you enlightened?

A few months ago, somebody asked me that question.

It's kind of fun to ponder the idea. Answering it begs the question, what is enlightenment? If I had it, how would I know? And what good would it do me? What is the opposite of enlightenment? And is there anything wrong with that?

The world has been home to many people we regard as enlightened. We've had the Buddha, Jesus, Muhammad, Mildred Norman and many others both celebrated and anonymous. The ones who shared their enlightened insights taught love, compassion and faith in an unseen power for good in the Universe. I try to be like them, but I don't beat myself up when I fail. None of them solved all the world's problems. All of them together didn't end world hunger or stop all wars. They did what they could. I do what I can.

When I was asked if I am enlightened, I can't remember exactly how I responded. I think I said something diplomatic and safe, something like, I have my moments of awareness. I didn't want to say I'm not enlightened. But I'm not foolish enough to come right out and say, "Oh hell yes. I'm the pinnacle of spiritual attainment." Too much responsibility comes with that.

The questions would only get harder. It's better I think to give myself some wiggle room. It's better I think to just be happy. It's better I think to be able to play around in the dark.

When I was a little boy, I would frequently stay overnight at my best friend Brian's house. He, his little sister and I would often play in the basement. And one of the games we enjoyed was turning off the lights, sneaking around and scaring the bejesus out of each other. The basement was large, and his parents kept it clean. But there was still a lot of stuff down there—lots of obstacles and nooks and crannies in which to hide. We knew our way around well enough that we never got hurt around his father's tools. The game often ended with us tickling and giggling in the soft safety of the laundry pile.

Next door to Brian lived a family with a couple boys around our age. Their names were Mike and Ricky. We often played with them too. Their father owned a little restaurant called DJ's Coffee Cup. Sometimes we rode our bicycles downtown to mooch hamburgers and soda. On one of those trips, there were about six of us. That many boys at one time was over the mooch limit. We were too disruptive to sit at the counter in the dining room, so Mike and Ricky's dad told us to go away.

Mike led us down a hallway toward the back door, but instead of leading us outside, he took us to the basement of the restaurant. It was cluttered with leftover stuff from businesses that had previously been there. Among the clutter, bolted to the floor, was a barber's chair. When we got bored exploring the old bare shelves and discarded signs that were strewn about, we started spinning each other in the barber chair. As the game evolved, we somehow all squeezed into or clung onto the chair, and we managed to get it spinning wildly. Suddenly, the lights went out.

The basement of the store didn't have any windows. We were in total darkness, and because we were spinning so wildly, we were completely disoriented. When we managed to stop the chair from spinning, we didn't know which way the door was. It wasn't like playing in Brian's dark basement. It was really quite frightening until Mike, groping, managed to find something familiar and feel his way to a light switch.

That experience spoiled the restaurant basement as a place to play. There was something ominous about being disoriented in absolute darkness. Still, playing in the dark in Brian's basement kept its charm. Here's the difference. In Brian's basement, even with all the lights turned off, there was a faint gray glow at each of the basement windows. Even playing in the dark, we always knew where we were. We always knew where the light switch was. And of course, we always knew that Brian's parents were right upstairs. We could hear them walking around, and we knew if we called for them, they would come.

I think we all have enlightenment sometimes—some more than others. I think many of us drift in and out of it—both by accident and at will. I think that the Buddha, Jesus, Muhammad and Mildred Norman drifted in and out of enlightenment too. Everybody has times when they are just too tired or hungry or lonely to have infinite compassion and absolute faith. And sometimes, it's just fun to play in the dark.

Sometimes, I think it's okay to simply know that enlightenment is available. Go ahead and play in the dark. Just play safely. Remember to meditate. That is like knowing where the windows are. Remember the presence and power of God. That is like knowing there are loving parents upstairs. Recognize the miracles of life. That is like hearing those parents walking around. Don't let yourself spin wildly out of control like a bunch of unsupervised little boys in an old barber chair. Instead, keep track of where the light switch is; that is, remember to pray.

I once read that enlightenment is not a destination but a tool to make the journey easier. Lately, I've been enjoying a pretty pleasant journey. Maybe that means I've drifted into enlightenment. But if I have, I will not tell you. I would rather reserve the right to play around in the darkness. I know how to turn on the light.

If you didn't notice, I tossed you a teaser. I didn't expect you to know who Mildred Norman was. But she was a remarkable woman, a 20th-century-American enlightened woman, who probably wouldn't want me saying that. She would probably rather that I tell you to live in peace knowing that life is good, and there is fun to be had everywhere—as long as you know where the light is—and it is inside you. And so it is.

HOW TOUGH ARE YOUR ISSUES?

Got issues? We all have them. They lurk in the dark doorways and corners of our minds like assassins waiting to bring us down. They strike with deadly accuracy because they know our patterns and weaknesses.

Lately, I've been thinking about how I handle them. Sometimes I ignore them. Sometimes I nurture them. Sometimes I entertain them. Sometimes I make them my Gods.

Then sometimes, I claim my power over them, and they willingly get out of my way. I know a lot of methods for claiming my power. Today, I'm thinking about one of them. It involves aligning myself with a power greater than my issues. It involves aligning myself with God.

When I was in seventh grade, I was smaller than most of the other kids. Middle-school-aged boys are very aware of things like that. Knowing I was vulnerable made me afraid. And knowing I was vulnerable made some of the other boys aggressive. I got chased and tormented. When I got a paper route and had money, I got shook down and threatened. Packs of thirteen-year-old extortionists would ambush me and demand candy bar money. It was torture. I learned to be evasive. I always had to change the way I moved in, around, to and from school. I was always looking over my shoulder. I lived with a lot of fear.

During the summer after seventh grade, a new kid moved to town. His name was Steve. I met him because he took over a paper route near mine. We picked up our newspapers every day at the same time in the same place. We loaded up our canvas bags and walked to our routes together. Like me, he was preparing to enter eighth grade. But he was different. He was a little bit bigger than most of the kids my age. He was a lot tougher. He was from a city where he had been in a rough crowd. He smoked. He shaved. And he was fearless. Even the toughest kids in my hometown seemed like helpless children compared to Steve. He never had to fight because everyone knew who would win.

In September, Steve and I walked to school together. In the afternoon, we walked to our paper routes together. I felt much more comfortable than I had the year before. I never told Steve about the kids who had picked on me then. He wouldn't have done anything. He would have just told me to do something about it. He felt confident taking care of himself. He figured everyone else should be able to do the same. Still, having Steve as a friend made me bully proof. Everyone stayed out of his way.

One day, Steve didn't come to school. As I was walking home in the afternoon, I happened upon three boys who had tormented me the year before. They were standing on the sidewalk ahead of me. As I was considering how I was going to dodge them—and keep my dignity intact—an interesting thing happened. The whole pack moved off of the sidewalk and across the parking lot. From in front of the Baskin Robbins store one of them called a taunt to me: "You think you're so tough because you hang around with that Steve Dresbach, and he smokes."

The truth was, I did. I felt tough. I wasn't getting picked on because I had made a powerful ally. I still feel smug just thinking about it.

This story illustrates a spiritual principle best stated in a wonderful quotation by Reverend Johnnie Coleman of Chicago, who tells her congregation, "When you're dealing with issues, don't tell God how big your problems are. Tell your problems how big your God is."

If I would have told Steve about the bullies, he wouldn't have done anything. But the bullies knew about Steve, so they fled.

Our issues behave the same way. They exist as little gangs of thoughts. They team up with feelings to make themselves seem more powerful. Some of them are clear, conscious memories—standing on the sidewalk blocking our paths. Some are repressed—hiding around corners to ambush us. They are all very real, and as long as we allow it, they are powerful. They have lives of their own. They trick and torment us. We can try to avoid them, and sometimes we succeed. But eventually, they find us.

Sometimes, we nurture them. They love it when we pull them out and share them with well meaning friends who say, "Oh you poor thing. You had it so rough." Sometimes, we entertain them. They are amused when we fall to our knees and beg God to make them go away. They laugh at our impotence.

When we focus upon them, we make them our Gods. Basic Science of Mind states that the One Universal Spirit that expresses Itself through each of us has given us the power to pray without ceasing, and whatever we place our attention upon grows in our experience. God is wherever our attention is.

This is not to say we should take all attention off of our issues. Remember they are lurking, waiting to ambush. But once we have identified them, we can let them know clearly and certainly that from now on, we are traveling with a power greater than theirs.

You see, issues are bullies, and bullies are cowards. Our issues are based in fear; therefore, they are made of fear. They are fear itself. That is all we really need to know. When our issues try to rear their ugly heads, we can declare our sovereignty over them. We are expressions of God. We all have our bullies that want to taunt us. But we all have a friend who is unquestionably tougher than all of the bullies put together.

I invite you to call out your issues. Dare them out of their hiding places. Then parade your God before them. Watch them flee. This may not be the only tool you need to conquer your issues, but it is a powerful one—because you are power. And so it is.

WAITING ON A SHADOW

Groundhog Day has come and gone—Punxsutawney Phil rolled away the stone, stepped triumphantly into the light, and said, "Go to hell. It's cold out here." And the peace sign of blue Christmas-tree lights is still burning on my front porch. It was supposed to be a Christmas decoration (the peace sign, not the groundhog). I was going to take it down on Saturday. Then I watched the news, and I couldn't bring myself to touch it. Christmas season is over. Peace season is having trouble making its appearance.

As I watch the news I wonder where people find the time and the motivation to fight with each other. I have trouble finding time to put my books away. The warriors of the world must use their Franklin Planners. I write tasks on Post-it notes that end up being used as bookmarks. I would suck at fighting a war. I procrastinate too much.

I recognize that there is a power for good in the Universe. I know that we are expressions of that power. I know It responds to us at the level of our beliefs. And by training my mind and shaping my beliefs, I gather the power of the Universe to shape my life.

This is quite simple in theory. And I know it works in practice. So to sit here and declare that I procrastinate runs contrary to effective spiritual practice. I know that, but the way I combat my self-defeating beliefs is to hold them up in the light. I spend a lot of time doing that. I have a reason.

Most of the beliefs that have a negative impact on my experience are hidden deep within the caves of my subconscious mind. They hide there like terrorists, waiting to make secret strikes when my guard is down.

In the years that I've been searching out these hidden enemies, I've made some great progress. I routed out the events of my life that made me feel ashamed. I pored through my past and found all the insults that were hurled at me. I dug up failures dating back to early childhood. I isolated all of these memories, so they could harm me no more. But I still find myself doing things that hold me back—having experiences of decline when I expect growth. Obviously, there are still enemies lurking within.

One of the spiritual mind treatments I find myself returning to is for understanding. I can't grow unless I know what is preventing it. I pray to understand. God answers all prayers. So as I gathered with the family at Christmastime, my mother gave me a clue as to where I must look next. I was talking about my new passion for golf. Something I said triggered a memory for her. She was almost angry. She said, "I used to get so mad at your father and all his golfing. I told him, 'You have other priorities. You have a son.' But he had a European mindset. He thought that the mother should take care of the kids."

I said, "Hmm," which is what I usually say to people when they rant, and I don't feel prepared to join them. I just wanted a warm and fuzzy Christmas. But I remembered what she said. It was about me. I had something to learn from it. Later a memory emerged.

One summer when I was about nine years old, I got interested in baseball. I didn't like playing at the park with the other kids because I wasn't any good. But I wanted to be. I wanted to learn. My favorite thing was playing catch with my father in the back yard. He would throw the ball so I could catch it. He'd warn me what he was going to do, so I could be prepared. He would announce "pop-up" or "grounder," and he would toss the ball in my direction. Then he would comment on my moves like a sportscaster. I also liked throwing the ball back to him. I would pitch it with all my might, and I was most pleased when he complained that catching it had hurt his hand. If he had been there, I would have played that game every afternoon. But he wasn't always there.

He started work very early every morning. Every afternoon, I expected his green Pontiac station wagon to come crunching up the gravel driveway at about 3:30. With my baseball and both of our fielders' gloves, I would wait at the picnic table in the back yard. I would daydream, and I would wait.

Once I saw an old western on TV. The Indians had captured a cowboy, and they were going to execute him. In the movie, one of the Indians jabbed a spear into the ground and announced that when the shadow reached a certain point on the ground, the white man would be killed. I don't remember what happened next. The cowboy was probably rescued. Western-movie conflicts were usually pretty tidy for the white guys. But the image of tracking time by the movement of a shadow got stuck in my imagination.

Waiting for my dad at the picnic table, I devised a solar-divination system. I would open my Cub-Scout knife, plunge the blade into the tabletop and proclaim, "When shadow reach first knothole, Dad be home." But my divination was flawed. As the shadow passed its designated point, I'd push out the deadline. "When shadow reach crack, Dad be home." "When shadow reach table edge, Dad be home." By the time he did get home, the shadow of the house usually covered the table and was growing across the back yard. It would either be time for supper, or he would be exhausted and want a nap.

I was a stoic little Indian. I hid my disappointment.

Now as an adult, I'm not angry with him. He had his own experiences that shaped the way he was. He was the son of Dutch colonists in Indonesia. He didn't talk about it much, but being a colonist would have made him an only child among a privileged minority. I'm sure loneliness and childhood were synonymous to him. When he was twelve years old, he was separated from his parents and placed in a concentration camp. His mother was placed in a women's camp. His father was sent to Burma to be a prisoner/slave on the Chinese-Burma railway. That was World War II. My dad was in the camp until he was fifteen.

If my dad was golfing when I wanted to play catch, I forgive him. He was cheated out of many early-life experiences. He had lost time he needed to recover. He had games he wanted to play. But that doesn't diminish the sadness of a little boy patiently watching the afternoon shadow of a Cub-Scout knife stretching across a picnic table. It doesn't alter the belief it left hidden in a secret cave of my mind.

I must now look at my aversion to Franklin planners. I have to look at my seemingly infinite capacity to procrastinate. As I leave a Christmas peace sign burning on my porch into February, am I really advocating peace, or am I waiting for my father to get home to help me take it down? As I tuck Post-it notes listing unfinished chores into unfinished books, am I pushing out the deadline of a creeping shadow? Is my patience in trying to grow a Sunday congregation a product of enlightened meditation, or is it an incredible, unhealthy capacity to wait without fulfillment?

Asking questions like these is part of my spiritual practice. It is learning to understand the shadows of the mind. I will never erase the dark memories that shaped the parts of myself I want to change. They are like shadows. They are not really part of me, but they follow wherever I go. I cannot run from them. They will only disappear when I expose them to the light.

The peace sign on my front porch means several things. The fact that it is still burning means I procrastinate. But the spirit of it is still sincere. It still means I advocate world peace. It also means I want peace within my own heart.

The reason I wonder how people find time to go to war is because I'm so busy fighting the war within myself. I know that my only real enemies are the shadow beliefs that hide beyond my awareness. I know I will only find peace when I track them all down. So I gather intelligence and hunt them. When I find them, I place them in secure areas where they can pose no threat. And I think that all of the warriors of the world are trying to do the same thing. They simply haven't figured out where the enemies are. They are looking the wrong way. They blame their pain and their fears on other people. They try to conquer each other just as I try to conquer the enemies that lie within.

I've had a few friends tell me to leave my peace sign on the front porch until we have world peace. I don't think that I will. I have to know that I'm not procrastinating. I'll take it down for now. I'll put it up again next Christmas. Or maybe I'll put it up again in a month. Time will tell. For now, it has done its job. It has sent its message to thousands of people who have driven past and seen it. But the fact is that peace on earth will only come when people discover that the enemies are within their own hearts.

GOODBYE CHARLIE

Spring is here. Charlie won't see it. Charlie was my neighbor. Last week, Charlie breathed his last. Two years ago, he painted my garage. For the last six months, he struggled against bone cancer. Now he's gone. He didn't have many interests. He didn't have many friends. His kids ignored him until the last few months of his life. He didn't like movies. He played a little bingo, watched a little TV and smoked like a damp campfire.

He never had much to say. Mostly, he liked to work. Jan never referred to him as her boyfriend or her man or her love. She always just called him her handy man. He kept her house and yard perfectly trim and tidy. He made wooden cutouts of cartoon characters, painted them, and put them out to populate the flower gardens. When he finished cutting the grass and trimming the trees and bushes, he carefully cleaned the bottom of the lawnmower and wiped off the clippers before he carefully put them exactly where they belonged in the garage. Then with the hose, he washed the excess clippings off of the sidewalk.

Perhaps because he was so tidy, Charlie didn't care much for Tootsie and Willy. They are Jan's dogs. They would always dig in or mess upon Charlie's work. That's what dogs do. Charlie wasn't mean to them. But he ignored them, and they ignored him. His life seemed very empty when he didn't have any chores to do.

As Jan told me about Charlie's last hours, I was struck by the way Spirit works in our lives. Two years ago, when Charlie was painting my garage for $300, Jan got it in her head that she should find a part-time job. She and Charlie were both retired. She said she didn't need the money, but she really felt she needed the activity. She wanted to learn something new and meet some new people. Since she loves her dogs so much, I tried to get her a job as a dog sitter with a friend who owns a pet-sitting service. But somehow, Jan and my friend just never managed to connect. They exchanged messages for about a month, and Jan lost interest. She thought about getting a job at a grocery store, but that didn't really appeal to her. She was feeling called, but she wasn't sure what was calling.

Then one day, I was out saying "Hi" to Tootsie and Willie, and Jan hurried to the fence all excited. She decided what she was going to do. She had registered as a hospice volunteer, and she was reading through the pamphlets that described the training she would receive. I think she read them through about five times, and the training was still two weeks away. I wanted to help her keep fuel on her fire, so I loaned her my Elisabeth Kubler Ross books. She loved them. I was happy for her. It was the most excited I'd seen her since Charlie made the Sylvester and Tweety cutouts that were in her front yard.

After that, when I would meet Jan at the fence, she would tell me about her progress as a hospice volunteer. She found it very rewarding. She had some tough assignments. She helped quite a few people live out their last days in the dignity and comfort of their own homes. Neither she nor I suspected that the Universe had called her to prepare her for the most difficult assignment of all—saying good-bye to her own handy man.

When Charlie was diagnosed six months ago, the doctors said his cancer had advanced too far to be cured.

They treated him the best they could. They tried to replace one of his hips, but the bone was so deteriorated that there was nothing to attach to. That's when he became confined to a wheelchair. The doctors thought he would have to spend his remaining weeks in the veteran's hospital, but Jan told them she was taking him home. She knew how to take care of him. She had her hospice-volunteer certification to prove it.

So Charlie spent his last few months in the living room. Jan took care of him, but she also had to take care of everything else. When she was in the basement doing laundry or outside shoveling snow, Charlie had the TV and Willie the dog to keep him company.

Tootsie is a young dog. She's only about 3, and she's still sort of antsy. Willie is a very old dog. He belonged to Jan's parents who both passed in the last five years. Tootsie is an attention-seeker. Willie is more of a lonely, old orphan. He's short and tubby and waddles around slowly. He was already old when his original humans passed on. Since then, he has mostly kept to himself. When Charlie moved into a hospital bed in the living room, Tootsie wasn't very interested. Charlie didn't play with her when he was up and around, so she saw no potential for fun with him in his weakened condition. But Willie seemed to understand something greater.

When Charlie got sick, Willie adopted him. They still didn't interact much, but Willie took a post near the foot of Charlie's bed and spent hours just being there. Jan said it was the strangest thing. And what Jan really found interesting was Willie's behavior last Monday. As Charlie's body was slowly failing and his soul was preparing to leave, Willie climbed up onto the blue chair beside Charlie's bed. This was no small feat. Willie is so old, short and tubby, it's all he can do to get up the few stairs between the back door and the kitchen. One stair is about 8 inches. The seat of the blue chair is twice that. But Willie somehow climbed up. It was the first time he ever got up on the furniture. Jan let him stay. She knew that Willie knew where he needed to be.

For the last four hours of Charlie's life, Willie stood watch over him. That same Spirit that called Jan to learn to be a hospice volunteer called Willie to see Charlie on his way. Even though Charlie and Willie were never close, their souls were. Spirit loves Spirit. Souls love souls. And when their old, failing bodies could no longer have their differences, Willie's soul and Charlie's soul reached out to touch one another. That is what Life wants to do.

Life is all about Love. We didn't come here to wash the lawnmower and paint garages. Life doesn't care if the hedge is trimmed and the grass clippings are washed from the sidewalk. Life doesn't care if we're short and tubby and old. Life just wants to Love.

After Jan told me about Charlie passing and Willie staying with him, she told me about her hospice visits of the last week. She told me about Sister Ann, who is 82 years old and gets tired of the food she is given. Jan smuggled her some low-fat cherry yogurt, and Sister Ann said she had never tried yogurt before. But she added, "That will be so good for my bones." And even though Jan's eyes were filled with tears from thinking about Charlie, she broke into a smile that warmed my heart and told me that she is going to be okay. Charlie is gone, but others still need her kindness. Jan has not stopped Loving. Jan has not stopped Living.

I know tomorrow as she goes outside to pick up after Tootsie and Willie, Jan will be thinking about Charlie. But she will also be thinking about Sister Ann and all the others whose lives she is touching. In that frame of mind, she will surely remember to appreciate the beginning of spring. And so must I. And so it is.

CHURCH OF THE GREEN

I'm a kook. This is my professional, ministerial assessment. The behavior that led to this diagnosis is a new obsession that I have. It is not a terribly harmful obsession. I don't think I have a problem yet, but I'm certainly keeping a watchful eye on myself. You see, I've begun to golf.

I have a lot of friends who golf. They would probably argue that there is no such thing as a golf problem. But I also know people who drink who think there is no such thing as an alcohol problem. This is not to say that I've developed a golf addiction (yet). But it seems quite strange to me that after almost 30 years of golf aversion, I should suddenly find myself wanting to sneak out of work early just to sink expensive little white balls in streams or ponds—or send them rattling off into the forest. But that is what I do.

Of course, I have my successes too. Occasionally, I step up to the tee and sail a perfectly straight shot 180 yards down the middle of the fairway. I think that is what keeps me going back. With every hook, slice or topped ball, I find myself knowing that I could have done better. I find myself remembering all of the little rules about elbows, hips, eyes and follow-through, and a little voice deep inside calls, "Do-overs." And I hoist my bag of clubs and head off for one more try. Something inside remembers my successes, and like the Little Engine That Could, I chug up the fairway thinking, "I know I can. I know I can." Something inside me knows I can golf a perfect game because something inside me knows that the perfection of Spirit is at the core of my being.

That sort of explains why I keep going back, but it does not explain why I started golfing in the first place. For years, I scoffed at golf. I condemned it as a feeble excuse for a sport and a waste of time and money. For years, I scoffed at people who golf. Now I am one. And it's not just something I do casually—like taking a yoga class or going to a movie. I'm becoming a golf kook, and it seems to have come upon me all of a sudden.

Perhaps it is a sign of maturity. For years, I was content to frustrate myself obsessing over beautiful women. Maybe golf is just the next phase. But that doesn't ring true. I still feel adequately obsessed with beautiful women—even while I'm golfing—so it is not as if golf is a replacement obsession.

Perhaps it is a healing. In spite of my years of scoffing at golfing, there is golf in my past. When I was a teenager, I golfed with my father.

His golfing was not generally a family activity. Some evenings, he would take my sister and me to the driving range to play miniature golf while he practiced his swing, but usually golf was something he did on weekends with other men. To me, his golfing was competition for his attention. I think he sensed that, so when I got big enough to walk the course, he started taking me along as his caddy. I got to pull his cart and see the game, but it was still not private time with him.

When I was about fourteen, he had gotten good enough to buy a nice set of clubs. He gave me his old clubs and started teaching me the game. For a few summers, we went out together to the VFW Pitch and Putt in New Berlin or to Edgewood, which was still under construction in Big Bend. Of course, he still went out with his friends on Sunday mornings while I was forced to go to Sunday school, but at least I was sharing some time with him. Until I started golfing this year, I'd practically forgotten the times with my dad.

When I was sixteen, and I turned into a raging bundle of hormones, I lost interest in my father. I got interested in girls and cars. When I was seventeen, I also developed an interest in alcohol and drugs. My relationship with my father turned very tense. Several weeks after my 18th birthday, I moved out of my parents' home. Four months after that, my father died.

He was only forty-two. It wasn't supposed to be that way. Even as I was living a dangerous life immersed in drug culture, I assumed I would grow out of it. And I assumed that my father and I would be adults together. I assumed we would go golfing, have a few beers, have a few laughs . . .. I assumed he would be there to watch me become whatever it was I was going to become. And he left. And I was angry. It wasn't supposed to be that way. And now I'm forty-six. I'm older than my father ever got to be. I think I've finally found what I am supposed to do with my life. And now I golf.

I feel my father's presence every time I step onto the course. I feel him watching my form when I tee off. I hear him advising me to adjust my grip, turn my clubface in, keep my head down, and follow through.

When I'm driving home from the golf course after a day of noticeable improvement, I find myself feeling terribly sad and wondering, "What's the point?" He's not around. I can't show him what I'm doing. I can't ask him for tips on my stance or my swing. I'm never going to win a round against him and have him tell me I did a good job. And I think that points to some of the reasons that I'm golfing now. I've come to know I must live for myself. I've come to know that among all my teachers, I am the one who will have the most impact upon me. I've also grown strong enough in feeling my feelings that I can finish grieving. To do that, I must recall my father by re-creating moments that represent him.

Those are the healing aspects of this re-discovered interest, but they do not explain the obsession. I think there is something even deeper going on. I feel like I'm golfing as a spiritual practice.

Golf is a sort of meditation. On the golf course, there is nothing to do but golf. It doesn't pay to worry about the chores that aren't getting done. The rustle of the breeze in the trees, the smell of the closely cropped grass and the sounds of frogs and splashing balls in the pond all fill my senses. It is easy for me to be fully present in the moment. It is a place where I can hear the voice of God. The goal of golf is to complete the course with the fewest number of strokes. The reward of being the winner goes to the person who finishes with the least effort.

Swinging the clubs is a lot like prayer. It requires focused concentration. The quality of the stroke is determined by accuracy rather than effort. In fact, just as in prayer, when swinging the golf club, effort defeats itself. A good swing requires keeping one's eyes on the ground. When the club strikes the ball, the golfer must have faith that the ball is going where it should. If the golfer loses faith and looks up, the ball goes nowhere. But if that should happen, the golfer always gets another turn. The final beauty of the game is that no matter how poorly one might do, everyone who plays can keep swinging until the ball finally rolls into the hole.

And that is the way it is with life. It unfolds however it will. We can improve the way we live when we keep trying, keep making adjustments, and keep practicing. We can't do it for anyone else. Each person is on his or her own path. People pass from our lives. We can't make them the reason we play the game. No matter how many mistakes we make, we can keep playing until we reach the goal, then we can say, "Do-overs" and try once more. So on top of all my other little quirks and eccentricities, I am now a golf kook. I use it for healing. I use it for spiritual practice. Maybe I even use it to commune with the spirits of departed loved ones. That's one of those things that can't be proven, but it is fun to think about—like golfing and beautiful women and God and of course, like you—because you are wonderful. And so it is.

BECOMING WHOLE

Crushes suck. And so it is.

That's it. Enough said. Crushes suck. But I should probably try to qualify that. Everybody experiences crushes a little differently. I've heard some people say they love them. They delight in the fanciful longing for some unattainable beauty or Adonis and will pass idle minutes dreaming of what can't be. That's not what I'm talking about. When I say, "crush," I'm talking about that all-consuming obsession that disguises itself to the sufferer as love. I'm talking about single-minded emotional dependence upon one particular person. I'm talking about an addiction. I'm talking about a burning desire that is so focused that it feels that only the object of the obsession can put the fire out. What I'm talking about sucks. I've been told that even married people get crushes. Children get crushes. Old people get them too. If you've never had one, add that to your gratitude list. If you don't have a gratitude list, start one.

I don't have a crush right now. But I have had many. Too many. And now I'm near a person who has one, and I can feel the pain. I can feel the confusion. I want to do something to help, but I know I can't. I know the feelings too well. And I suddenly see something I've never understood before. It is something I've been told. I'm not having an original insight here. But I've always had it explained while I was suffering under the weight of full-blown crushes. Those were not the most lucid times of my life.

Now, the Universe has offered me the opportunity to observe. I'm on the outside of a crush looking in, and I see myself. It is now clear to me what I could have learned all along. I guess I wasn't ready. Or maybe I was too distracted or too close too the pain. In any event, I better learn it now. I don't want to suffer another crush if I can avoid it. The lesson—the thing I was told but never grasped—was that when I had a crush, I saw in the object of my desire a quality I felt I was lacking. Each timeI had a crush, I wanted her—whomever she happened to be that time—to make me whole by bringing that quality I felt I lacked into my life. Do you get it?

I can think of at least seven crushes in my adult life. Looking back, every one of them fit the pattern. Every one of them held the lesson. Every time, I could have avoided the pain, and there was a lot of it. Sometimes it went on for years.

First crush, five years. I remember when it began. I remember when it ended. I was seventeen years old. She was fifteen. I was struggling to become mature by emulating the greasy men with whom I worked at Don's Service Center. I worked fifty hours a week. I had black fingernails. I cussed. I hung out at the bowling alley. I adopted strong judgments and opinions. I tried to fit in among hard-drinking mechanics and truck drivers. I drank a lot.

One night at a party, there she was. She was kind of quiet, and very pretty with blond hair and blue eyes. But the thing that struck me, though I probably didn't know it then, was her youthful innocence. She wasn't trying to impress anyone by showing off her new maturity the way the rest of us were. She simply sat wide-eyed and took it all in. I saw something I'd lost. I wanted it back. I needed her to give it to me. We went out for a few months. Then one day, I was on my way to the auto-parts store in the gas-station pick-up truck. I felt like a big shot. I stopped by the high school. It was just after lunch. I knew she would be outside with her friends. I pulled up, rolled down my window, held court for a few minutes and got ready to drive away. Rather than give me a kiss, she said, "We need to talk."

I'd never gotten that line before, but I knew what it meant. I was half panicked the rest of the day. My boss watched me put snow tires on the front wheels of a rear-wheel drive sedan. He just looked me in the eye and asked, "What's her name?" He knew. He'd been there. A year later when he fired me for always being screwed up on drugs and alcohol, he probably didn't know I was still burning for her. It wasn't what gas-station mechanics talked about. But I hurt. I hurt for a long, long time. The pain did not go away until I was 23. I came home on leave from the Navy. I had changed. So had she. I ran into her at the university where I was visiting a friend. She was still pretty, but she no longer had what I needed. Perhaps traveling the world helped me regain a sense of wonder. Or perhaps she no longer projected that same innocence that I'd been drawn to before. Most likely, a little bit of each. Life is rarely "this" or "that."

A few years later, I got a new crush. I was still in the Navy. She was a civilian. I was lonely and unhappy. She radiated joy. I would see her at the grocery store where she worked and where I bought beer. Or I would see her around town, going to the drugstore or to the bank with her little daughter in tow. She had strawberry blond hair and green eyes. She was always smiling, and anyone who saw her had to smile too. We talked about going out, but it never happened. I drank too much. She knew it. She sold me my beer. I ached to have her make me whole. Of course, she could not. It never occurred to me that I must find my joy within. When I got out of the Navy, I returned to Wisconsin.

I started college when I was twenty-seven. First semester, new crush. I was still drinking hard. I'd grown spiritually empty and agnostic. I was attracted to a woman with dark hair and brown eyes in my Com 101 class. She told the class that she was religious with old-fashioned values. That was what I wanted from her. That time, I think I knew it, but I didn't consider cultivating those qualities in myself. We went out for a short time, and then she started avoiding me. I left messages and wrote long, maudlin letters to her, praising her for her goodness and her beauty and begging her to be part of my life. I kept that up until I found out she was pregnant. That ruined my fantasy.

The next one was a woman who was driven by long-term goals as I was living day by day with no sense of purpose.

The next one was vivacious and self-assured while I was introverted and shy. Time went on. I got busy in a high-tech career. I was living in a cubicle, scheduling in a day-planner and eating nothing but processed foods. So I developed a crush on a woman whom I perceived as living simply. She had dog fur all over her clothes. She ate meals prepared from fresh ingredients. She was down to earth. I wanted her to ground me.

Like all the others before, this was a crush that dragged on for years. I was obsessed and gloomy. My friends got tired of hearing about it. And I could not understand how this person whom I adored could not feel the same way about me. I hounded her. I tried to manipulate her with carefully crafted letters. I tried praise, patience and guilt. Nothing I did could make her make me whole—because she could not make me whole. All of the years I've wasted, I could have lived fully if I had only known. If I could have recognized that my burning obsessions were not love, I might have been able to step back from my pain and see what it was that my heart was truly yearning for. Yes, these were all attractive women, but there are millions of attractive women on this planet.

The ones whom I was fixated upon had things I felt were lacking from my life. If I had seen—if I had known—I could have done what I needed to cultivate the qualities I yearned for within myself. I could have saved a lot of time. I could have avoided a lot of pain. I could have spent more of my life enjoying the wholeness that I truly am.

You see, I've always been whole. You have always been whole. It's the way we are made. We are expressions of God; therefore, we are whole, perfect and complete. It's just that sometimes, our thoughts or feelings or activities get out of balance. We put too much emphasis on certain aspects of ourselves at the expense of others. Then those neglected others cry out for expression. If we can learn the language of our hearts and souls, we can learn to interpret those feelings that make us search outside ourselves for a sense of wholeness. For some people, this would be a minor shift. For people like me—people with addictive personalities and a tendency to mistake painful yearning for love—it would be a spiritual transformation. So with this insight, I'm ready for the next time. As soon as I feel that unnatural yearning for someone to make me complete, I'm going to turn within. Instead of enduring the pain of having a crush on someone who cannot help me anyway, I'm going to try having a crush on God. I know it is a weird idea, but think about it. Every crush I've had came from a sense of something missing. But God made me whole. And God continues to make me whole. And what I send out to God is mirrored back to me. So if I give my heart and soul over to God, God will give my heart and soul back to me—whole, perfect and complete.

The form this will take will depend on what I choose. I know if I choose wisdom, God will guide me to wisdom. I know if I choose peace, God will guide me to peace. It's a different kind of obsession—a different kind of crush. It will not leave me feeling empty for years because unlike the crushes of my past, God can help. God makes me whole all the time. God does this for me, and God does this for you—because you are wonderful. And so it is.

LIFE IN A CAT HOUSE

I live in a cathouse. I'm surrounded. They've taken over. When I walk in the door, I'm greeted by four furry friends all mewing for attention, getting under my feet and climbing up my legs with razor-sharp claws. They crave my affection, and the competition is getting fierce.

I try to love them all—I do love them all—but each one wants my undivided love. When I stoop down among them and try to distribute my petting equally, each one seems to feel cheated. They want to be petted one-at-a-time. So they follow me around. They jump on the counters because they know that means getting picked up and carried to the kitty condo by the front window. They wait for me to sit, and they scramble up my chair to get onto my lap. I had to move a cat out of my office chair in order to sit down to write. Then I had to close the office door, or my lap would be full and little paws would be reaching for the keyboard. Juggling my affection has become a challenge.

I got Jean Louise in the summer of '89. She is a gentle and passive creature, and we lived comfortably together for four years. But I often worried that she needed company when I wasn't home. That probably wasn't true. The woman at the humane society told me that house cats are not pack animals, and a second cat would be more of a comfort to me than to Jean Louise.

But when a woman at work told me her college-student son had to find a home for his one-year-old neutered male, I thought it would be a good idea. I figured that a little one-year-old would not threaten Jean Louise's senior status.

My friend's son came over with a blue, plastic pet carrier. He placed the carrier on the living room floor and unhooked the front latch. I expected to see a little pink kitty nose poke tentatively out. Instead, it was like a scene from "Jurassic Park." The door of the carrier flew open, and out leapt a fearless bundle of muscle. He looked around predatorily (I smell cat. Where is she?), and boldly took over the house. That was how I got Murphy.

Murphy is abnormally large and aggressive. His roughhousing was somewhat stressful on meek Jean Louise. But they adapted. If I sat down in a chair, Murphy got my lap, but Jean Louise still owned the best part of the bed when we slept at night. Both their needs were being met. Then last Thanksgiving, one-eyed Meera joined the family.

Meera has brought a new set of challenges. She is small, but she lost her eye to something tougher than Murphy. She's not afraid to challenge his ownership of my lap, and she routinely chases Jean Louise from the bed.

Jean Louise would disagree, but I've found the tension manageable. I find cats to be curious, affectionate and funny. Having three has given me a lot of laughs. But I've also learned that three is enough.

A few Saturdays ago, I was pulling the weeds that had taken over the flowerbed next to the alley. It was about 100 degrees. I had sweat running in my eyes. But the weeds were so terribly out of control that I didn't want to postpone the job any longer. I was miserable. The sultry heat and still air made me feel stuck—as if the misery was permanent, and I was born to suffer. Then I heard a cat sound. It was a tiny squeak. I looked up from my work, and there was a little gray kitten peering at me through a rose bush. I said, "Hi," and she walked straight to me. I dropped my digging tool and picked her up in my dirty, sweaty hand. She was so small that my palm spanned her belly. Her tiny front legs hung down between my thumb and forefinger, and her little hind legs hung over against my pinky. She started to purr. It was all over. I forgot I was miserable. I left my tools and basket on the ground and carried her inside.

Of course, she's adorable. She plays and plays. Her favorite toy is attached to Murphy. He moans his complaints as the kitten delights in chasing and biting his big, fat tail. Because she is so tiny and cute, I've probably been favoring the kitten, which would explain why things are getting catty around here. Murphy, Jean Louise and Meera have not been aggressive toward the kitten, but they've all been aggressive for my attention. They are not being very nice to each other.

I have to sleep with the bedroom door closed, or there is a constant parade across my bed. At first I thought we could sleep in peace, but it was like sleeping in a bus station. Murphy lay thumping his tail against the dresser. Meera dragged all the cat toys onto the bed and crinkled the Mylar balls between her teeth. The kitten tried nursing on my ears and lips. She explored my nostrils, battled my hair and licked the corners of my eyes. Jealous Jean Louise went into hiding.

When I'm not in bed, I can barely walk through a room without stepping on a paw or a tail. The little one thinks I'm a tree made just for her to climb. On top of that, the cat food is disappearing at an alarming rate, and the litter boxes won't stay clean no matter how much I scoop. And I don't even want to think about all the fur.

This is a lesson about life. We all have things we enjoy. We all have things we are attracted to and things we are fond of. Every day brings new opportunities, new interests, new delights. We welcome them all. We nurture them all. Then suddenly we realize we've taken on too much. We try to juggle too much work with all of our hobbies and interests. We have to put our friends on the calendar and schedule appointments to relax with them. The things in our lives may all be good, but they all want our attention. And we can only pet one kitty at a time. We get too busy. We get overbooked, and we start losing sleep on account of it.

People like to accumulate. We tend to think that some is good, more is better and too much is just enough. But that isn't true. Too much is too much. And as long as we keep taking on new things, we have to find ways of giving other things up. But we can't give up the things that are dear to us, so we have to set priorities. I have to let go of a few of these cats. Jean Louise and Murphy have been here a long time. We've lived together for years. That means that, as cute as they may be, the youngsters have got to go. Fortunately, the Universe has a way of straightening things out. My friend who rescued Meera just bought a house, and her daughter wants a gray kitten. I just happen to have one, and I have a companion for her too. Next weekend, Meera and the baby are moving across town.

Jean Louise will be relieved. Murphy will miss roughhousing with Meera. I will probably miss all the antics. But we can't have it all. The late Dr. Kennedy Schultz used to say, "If we got everything we wanted, it would kill us." I can think of many times in my life when that was true.

But right now, I'm finding my comfort in the Zen saying, "Desire what you have." I have some curious, affectionate, funny, companions. I have the wisdom to let go of the ones to whom I can't give the attention they need. I have good friends who will give them a good home. I have a full and joyous life. I have food to eat and a roof over my head. I have a bed to sleep in—I hear it calling me now. And so it is.

WHERE IS YOUR MIND?

Where is your mind?

My teacher Reverend Vince used to ask that question of all his students. It was his way of reminding us to practice mindfulness. I remembered it today as I suffered the consequences of practicing mindlessness. I wasn't intentionally practicing mindlessness. I was just rushing. I was in a hurry to get to an appointment with the chiropractor.

My lower back has been troubling me. It started a few weeks ago. I have an old issue that I got tired of dealing with a few years ago. When I was working on it then, I had a lot of lower back pain. All of our emotional stuff finds places to lodge in our bodies. The issue I was dealing with likes to stick in my low back and hips. A few years ago, when I got tired of the back pain, I walked away from the issue. I quit dealing with it directly. The back pain went away. But at the same time, one of my feet went numb. It's been numb ever since—a reminder that there is something I'm in denial about feeling. Recently, I got tired of the numbness. I decided I needed to go back and finish dealing with the old issue. As soon as I did, the back pain came back, the same as it felt before.

I'm not saying that every pain is an unresolved issue. As Freud said, "Sometimes a cigar is just a cigar." But I am in touch with my body well enough to know when a pain or sensation is a physical manifestation of an emotional condition. That's what I have now. It is more than just a simple backache.

I'm seeing the chiropractor to minimize the discomfort, but I know the healing must take place in my consciousness. It's up to me to complete all the changes. But I couldn't do it alone before, so I'm getting a little extra help. In addition to seeing the chiropractor, I'm working with another type of therapist whom I may tell you about when I see results. And of course, I'm working on healing through sound spiritual practice—at least most of the time—but not this morning.

This past Saturday, I read a short essay on spiritual practice. The main idea of the essay is best expressed as a question. What could you possibly be doing that is more important than having your daily visit with God? I think it's a very good question. When I read it, I planned to ask it at church. I figured it would make me sound smart. It would make me sound spiritual. I could ask it at church with a very lofty tone in my voice. I would sound very authoritative. But I forgot to ask it at church. And it seems that this morning, I forgot about it altogether.

When I woke up today, it was pouring rain. That was as good a reason as any to hit the snooze alarm about four times. That takes a half hour out of my spiritual practice. I usually allow myself about an hour and fifteen minutes. That gives me a half hour to read and get woke up, fifteen minutes to pray, and a half hour for meditation. This morning when I finally got out of bed, I wondered how long the rain was supposed to last. So I logged onto the Internet to check the weather maps. And as long as I was logged on, I checked to see if I got any email overnight. That burned up another fifteen minutes. And because of wet roads, I figured I should leave the house about fifteen minutes early. That left me with fifteen minutes to read, pray and meditate.

So I logged off the computer, hopped into my meditation room, and jumped on the spiritual practice express. I went through the motions as quickly as I could, but it was not the real thing. It was shoddy spiritual practice, and I got proportionate results.

On mornings when I really give my attention to God, I step out of my back door with a deep sense of peace and security. On good days, I'm in love with all creation and I feel fully supported by Spirit.

This morning, I stepped out the door feeling harried. I clutched my briefcase under my arm trying to keep papers in the side pockets from getting wet. The moment I stepped into the torrential rain, it seemed to get heavier. I scooted back onto the porch to ponder my twenty-yard dash to the garage. I tried to assess whether the rain might subside soon, but it didn't seem promising. My mind started going to all the wrong places.

On a good day—on a mindful day—I would have been fully present with the rain. I would have been struck by the awesome beauty of the miracle that water can fall from the sky. I would have been aware of how good it was for the flowers and trees. I would have been at peace with the truth that the rain was falling at the speed of God and if I were late for my chiropractor appointment, it was because the Divine Mystery had perfect reasons for adjusting my schedule—reasons I may never know, but reasons that were perfect nonetheless. But I wasn't having a good day. I wasn't having a God day.

Standing on the porch, my mind raced back to my childhood. I thought about the period in my life from which all of my issues seem to have come. I spent my first few years of grade school having a perfect childhood experience. I was among the smartest kids in the class, so school was a delight. I must have been popular because it was never something I thought about. But those were days of educational experiments, and I became a guinea pig. I did so well in second grade that the school bumped me straight up to fourth grade to see how I would do there.

I suddenly found myself surrounded by kids who were a year older than me—kids who had the full benefit of attending third grade. I suddenly went from being the star of the class to being unable to keep up with the others. I was less developed socially, physically and academically. I often had to stay after school to try to get my work done. Walking home alone, I had to walk past the church where I went to Sunday school each week and sang, "Jesus loves the little children, all the children of the world . . ." But it didn't feel that way to me. I felt abandoned. I felt lonely and unsupported. And that was where my mind was as I stood on my porch watching the rain this morning.

A clap of thunder snapped me out of my daydream, and I realized I had to get moving, rain or no rain. I clutched my briefcase more tightly under my arm. I shrugged my shoulders up and pulled my chin down, like a turtle trying to hide his head, and I dashed for the garage. But I only made it two steps. When my feet hit the wet wooden stairs, they flew out ahead of me and I hit the edge of a stair with the exact part of my lower back that I was going to have treated at the chiropractor.

My briefcase had slipped from my grasp, and my papers were getting drenched. The buttons had torn loose from my raincoat and the heavy, cold rain was having its way with me. My sacrum throbbed and burned. And in my mind I heard two questions, "Where's your mind?" and "What could you possibly be doing that is more important than having your daily visit with God?"

I somehow managed to get up, sprint on one leg to the back alley and lift the garage door. Even through the pain, I could see meaning in the situation. When I begin my days communing with God, when I remind myself that I'm fully supported by an omnipotent loving presence, I move easily though my days—as if flying on the wings of angels. But today I went dashing off thinking about how I felt when it seemed the God of my childhood had abandoned me, and all my support slipped right out from under me.

That's the way life works. God is always present and will be whatever we expect It to be. The way God responds to us is determined by the way we respond to God. Throughout sacred texts the message is repeated over and over that it is done unto us as we believe. It is up to us to shape our beliefs to the way we want our lives to look. And that's why I asked: where is your mind?

You can choose to feel overwhelmed and unsupported, or you can approach life more wisely. You can remember that there is nothing more important than your daily visit with God. You can remember that God is always present everywhere—that God's support is your birthright—and you can move easily and joyously through one beautiful experience after another, which is what I hope you do—because you are wonderful. And so it is.

PRAY WITHOUT CEASING

I struggle with the concept of duality. Sometimes I wonder why I bother. I am having a sensory experience in which things are defined by their opposites. I understand cold because I have known hot. I understand light because I have known darkness. I recognize love because I have known loneliness. By these contrasts, I can only conclude that duality is a gift that gives meaning to life. Yet I struggle.

I've had the experience of transcendence. I've visited that psycho-spiritual realm in which opposites fall away, and I'm aware only of the absolute presence of God. It is an experience of Oneness, and going there helps me to more easily negotiate the experiences of duality that tend to be less innocuous than hot-cold, light-dark, love-lonely. I guess that's why I struggle. Among the sets of opposites that define the human experience are many that are illusory. They are opinions. They shift and bend to the influences of the moment. They give rise to conflict. Conflict raises a barrier between sensory experience and God.

This morning in my spiritual practice, a memory stirred. I managed to party away my twenties giving very little thought to God. I was agnostic mainly because it was convenient. If God was beyond knowing, I didn't need to try. My time was spent engaged fully in physical experience. The interesting thing was that I found my physical experience so painful that I concentrated most of my energy upon disengaging from it. Everything I did was focused around drinking and doing drugs. I lived in Southern California for part of that time. I never went to Disneyland because it wasn't a place to get drunk. When I went to movies, I always went to the drive-in because I could keep a cooler of beer in my back seat. Fishing was good. Bait stores always sold beer.

Needless to say, there were downsides to the way I lived. My money was always disappearing. My health was poor. My friendships were limited. But the biggest problem was one of which I wasn't even aware. I wasn't learning how to negotiate the opposites that defined my adult experience. When I had conflicting opinions, I clouded my mind. When I had conflicting feelings, I numbed my senses. I didn't learn how to manage anger and disappointment because I could cover them over. My answer to everything was, "Who cares?" Then I decided to sober up. I was thirty-two years old. My circumstances were crashing in on me. I had sacrificed most of my options, so it was time to try something new.

The first few months of living consciously were hellish. I found out how it felt to be me, and I didn't like it. Life felt ugly. Nothing happened the way I wanted, and I was forcing myself to experience what that felt like. I had a counselor who helped me through those days. I would go to her office and tell her of yet the latest unbearable dilemma to befall me. I sort of hoped she would prescribe a six-pack or give me a pill that would fix me. But that wasn't her job. She only offered me lousy little words of wisdom. She would tell me to look at conflicts and disappointments and say, "Who cares?" But I'd forgotten how to do that. The only prescription she offered was prayer.

When life was completely unfair and everybody and everything were conspiring to make me miserable, she told me to pray. When I was dismally lonely and misunderstood, she told me to pray. When the news was all bad and the entire government was either corrupt or misguided, she told me to pray. None of the problems I presented to her was too big for her crummy little prescription. All she knew how to do was tell me to pray. So eventually, I tried it. Funny thing was, it helped.

That was what I remembered this morning in my practice. In those days when I found almost every moment unbearable, mainly because I hadn't developed the maturity to accept life on its own terms, prayer helped. And I started using it constantly. When I was standing in line at the grocery store and the person at the checkout was holding everyone up arguing over an expired ten-cent coupon, I prayed. When it was pouring rain and I had two minutes to walk three blocks, I prayed. When I let the dog out and he was dawdling about doing his doody, I prayed. When I couldn't get to sleep at night, I prayed. Sometimes, the prayers I said seemed to change the conditions that upset me. Other times, the prayers changed me enough to accept conditions. It was the only tool I had, so I prayed without ceasing. And my prayers carried me out of the most difficult period of my life.

Things are different now. I've refined the way that I pray. I've also learned to live in greater harmony with the conditions of life, so I've refined what I pray about. This is good. But it has its downsides. Being comfortable with who I am takes away the urgency to pray. Being patient with things that used upset me has made me less likely to pray without ceasing. Instead of leaning upon God to carry me through the checkout line at the grocery, I just let it be what it is. I know I'll get where I need to be at the perfect speed of God. But deep inside, there is still a part of me that grows annoyed and anxious. Where negative feelings used to overwhelm me like a tidal wave, the same feelings now pass as a slight trickle. Prayer seems less necessary, but even a trickle can wear away a boulder over time. Every so often, I recognize I've ignored the trickle too long. A part of me that seemed solid and unmovable has worn down. If I could remember to pray without ceasing, I could stop even the trickle. That's why I struggle with duality.

My struggle is not to overcome duality but simply to remain conscious of it. Overcoming duality—moving into transcendent awareness—is not something that can be achieved by struggle. It is achieved in the silence of meditation. It can also occur spontaneously under the right conditions. But most of my hours are spent negotiating the duality of hot and cold or light and darkness and the shifting illusions of good and bad. If I want to enjoy better meditation—or if I want to increase the frequency of spontaneous transcendent experiences—I have to create the right conditions inside myself. I have to reconcile the sets of opposites that give my life definition. I can only do that through prayer.

This morning in my spiritual practice, I decided today I would pray without ceasing. I decided that I would include a prayer with every choice I made. Feed the cats—say a prayer. Walk to the garage—say a prayer. Drive to the office—say a prayer. Organize my activities—say a prayer for each and every one. My unfortunate discovery was that I've lost the consciousness to do that. By nine o'clock, I'd forgotten my commitment. I spent an average day having an average experience. I deserve better.

Through the years as I've refined the way that I pray, I've learned that the first step is to establish a heartfelt connection to God. Otherwise, a prayer is like talking at a telephone without dialing a number. Yesterday, I took a drive to Holy Hill. It is a sacred place. People go there to establish a heartfelt connection to God. I sat down in one of the many little chapels and immediately found myself in prayer. There was no duality, only the perfect oneness that transcends opposites. So maybe my answer is to give up the struggle. Perhaps as one grows in awareness of God, the rules change. Maybe the reason I don't pray without ceasing in the world of opposites is that I no longer have to. But I want to. I want to consciously include God in every step of my life. And perhaps the struggle with duality is a misguided attempt.

The truth is that I cannot escape God. Whether or not I'm remembering prayer, God is present. So perhaps I need to redefine my life. Rather than thinking of it as an exercise in reconciling opposites, maybe it's time to define myself as a prayer. God is just as present in the office as God is present at Holy Hill. The places I go throughout my day are the many chapels in which to establish heartfelt connection. Tomorrow in my spiritual practice, I will make the same commitment I made this morning. I will choose to pray without ceasing. I guess that's what I've been doing all along. My choice is to do it more consciously. And so it is.

Scott de Snoo

A DARK NIGHT OF A QUESTIONABLE SOUL

Yesterday, I was an atheist. It was Sunday. I wasn't an atheist all day. I got up in the morning to my spiritual practice. I did my readings and meditation, said my prayers, went to church and delivered my lesson, and I did it all in complete sincerity. When I lay down for my afternoon nap, I thought of God—as I always do while I'm going to sleep.

When I got up from my nap, I had chores to do. I had plans to rearrange some furniture and finish up some paperwork. But there is a lesson that I have to keep relearning. There is something lonely for me about Sunday afternoon. This has been true for many years. It probably goes back to my childhood when Sunday afternoon was a time to get together with grandparents, and Sunday evening was family time—time to watch "The Wonderful World of Disney," "The Ed Sullivan Show," and "Bonanza." Sunday was family time. Sunday meant love.

Now I am a single adult living alone. I have responsibilities and little free time. I see chores pile up, and I schedule the best I can. When I get behind, I look at the large chunk of personal time that comes after church each Sunday, and I imagine myself filling it by completing all the extra work I've accumulated through the week. But when the time comes, something inside me wants to be among other people. Something inside me craves the warmth and security of that family time I knew forty years ago. And when I don't get it, something inside me sends my mind straight to the gutter.

It begins with an empty feeling. When I give my attention to the emptiness, it calls me to fill it. So I look outside myself—I look to the family that isn't there. As I attend my emptiness, it turns to longing. Then it gets out of control. I tend to think about someone I wished I could have married. I start thinking "if only...." If only I'd have done this differently. If only I hadn't done that. If only she would call right now. If only.

"If only" is about the saddest place a person can go. I went there yesterday. And that was when I became an atheist.

When we don't get what we want—when life doesn't look the way we think it should—we tend to want to blame. And the most convenient scapegoat is God. So as I languished, I started to blame. But my understanding of God doesn't allow room for blame. I know God provides, but I also know that my consciousness provides the blueprint for God's provision. I am responsible for my experience.

As I languished in my loneliness, I knew that the answer was as far away as the telephone. I knew that nothing would change until I changed it. But it was too late. It wasn't too late by the clock. My friends are grown ups. They can make spontaneous choices. And I'm sure at least one of them was craving companionship just as I was. But it was too late because I had given myself over to the sadness. And I couldn't blame God. So I stopped believing.

I wanted a parent-God. I wanted a God that would have anticipated my emotional needs and provided the answer with no effort on my part. But no such God exists. So I decided that no God exists at all.

I thought about what my new life as an atheist would look like. I'd have the same job. I'd have the same house. I'd have many of the same interests. I'd pretty much be the same person; only I'd have more free time because an atheist certainly can't be a minister. That would be hypocrisy. I thought about whether I would treat people differently. There is a highly biased, illogical assumption in our society that people who don't believe in God have no moral foundation to their lives. I considered whether giving up God meant giving up my principles. But it did not. I knew as an atheist that I would still treat all people with kindness, compassion and respect. It's the right thing to do. And it has its own rewards.

I have atheist friends. They lead fulfilled lives. They are good people, and have genuine respect for the planet and for humanity. At the same time, I know of many other people who profess deep religious conviction and see nothing wrong with exploiting the planet or other people for their own personal gain. I tried to think of a news story about bloodthirsty atheists, or atheist terrorist organizations, or atheist intolerance. But I couldn't think of any. All the atheists I could think of are highly intelligent people making great contributions to humanity through scientific study and exploration. As far as I could tell, I was stepping into good company.

I tried imagining myself at ministers' conference next week announcing to my colleagues that I would have to pull out. I tried to imagine how they would respond when I said, "I've become an atheist."

I could only imagine them saying, "Oh. I know. I have days like that too."

Feeling separated from God is part of the human experience. We are sensory beings. We live in a world of sights and sounds— a world of tastes, textures and odors. We deal with gravity and temperature. We experience pain and suffering. We know hunger and exhaustion. We also experience comfort and pleasure, but no amount of either keeps us from getting old and dying. Feeling separated from God makes sense. Yet there is still something within us that senses an unseen presence. There is something that ponders the mysteries of intelligence and love. Even in the atheist, there is something that stands in awe at the splendor of creation, and as I pondered all these things, I thought, "I am a spiritual being having an atheistic experience."

Upon that thought, I said an atheist's prayer. I said it out loud—with cynicism and anger. I said, "Alright so-called infinite-mind-in-me-think-you're-so-smart. Last chance. Show me your stuff."

That made me feel better. I don't know why. It just did. I remembered a friend who frequently struggles with the same type of loneliness that I was feeling. I imagined her spending her Sunday playing solitaire on the computer with an eye on her Inbox hoping a message would come. So I wrote her a little note to let her know that she wasn't the only one. I told her how I was struggling with thoughts of that old, unrequited love of my past.

She responded a few minutes later. She wrote, "It is not the woman herself that you are pining over, it is your fantasy of who you think she is." My friend was right. I wasn't dealing with reality. So I wrote a few other notes to a few other friends and went to bed.

When I awoke this morning, I wasn't an atheist anymore. I thought of a little plaque that hangs in the kitchen of a Catholic institution I sometimes visit. The plaque reads, "Don't pray for an easy life; pray to be a strong person." So that was what I did.

Today at work, I talked with one of my friends. She is not a worrier, but she has some real concerns. She told me about her friend who is battling cancer as she takes care of a baby she just adopted. My friend also told me of another friend who has been over-working and isolating since losing a loved one to cancer a few months ago. There is much suffering in the world. It is not like the suffering I manufacture in my head when I spend Sunday afternoon alone. It is real suffering. I felt grateful that I could listen to my friend. It helped us both. We found comfort in the sharing. To me, it felt like family time. It gave me the sort of comfort I used to get watching "Ed Sullivan" and "Bonanza." But more importantly, it gave me a spiritual connection.

Our true nature is spirituality itself. We don't have to believe it, but it is there. We are spiritual beings having all the pain and suffering of a human experience, and we are also spiritual beings having the comfort and pleasure of a human experience. We can be Religious Scientist, agnostic, Christian, Muslim, or atheist, but we are all spiritual beings. Sometimes we feel it. Sometimes we don't.

This afternoon, I received an email from a woman. She just suffered a devastating loss. Her heart is broken. In her message she said she has given up on spirituality. She wanted me to take her off the list of people who receive my weekly spiritual messages. My heart goes out to her, and I'm not going to take her off the list. Yesterday, when I was an atheist, I determined that I would treat all people with respect. Now I am once again a man of God, and I am not going to respect that woman's right to leave this spiritual family—at least, not now.

Maybe I'm having an episode of spiritual pride. Maybe because I was an atheist just 24 hours ago, I'm having one of those annoying experiences of feeling I have to force my newly acquired spirituality on others. Maybe I'm a pushy control freak who wants to butt in on her private affairs. But this is the way it is this Monday night. You can call me disrespectful. You can even call me a sinner if you like. But I used to be an atheist. Now I've found God. And so it is.

Scott de Snoo

MY BIG BREAK

I'm celebrating an anniversary. Fifteen years ago, life as I knew it came to an abrupt end. It was not an unhappy ending, but it was traumatic at the time. For many years leading up to that turning point, I lived for my appetites. And some of those appetites were destructive.

My problem was that I didn't like myself. I didn't like the way I felt. I didn't like the way I looked. I didn't recognize my achievements. I didn't see any hope for improvement. Immersed in dissatisfaction, I drank. I took drugs. I clouded my awareness with any substance that could alter my mood.

Among other things, substance abuse is expensive. I was always out of money. This added to my shame. It also drove me to illegal activities to supplement my income. In an upstairs bedroom of a house I was renting, I had a garden. I grew mushrooms. They weren't the kind you would put on a pizza. They were hallucinogenic. Growing them was a lot of bother, but the work paid off at harvest time. I made more from selling them than I made at my full-time job. That kept me solvent. It also kept me in contact with the types of people who shared my devotion to mood altering substances. Being a drunken drug user surrounded by drunken drug users, I was able to convince myself that there was some sort of normalcy and validity in the way I lived.

Then one night—April 28th, 1987—there was a determined knock on my door at about two in the morning. It was the county drug-enforcement squad. There were about a dozen men. They had shotguns and a search warrant. That was my life-changing moment.

Interestingly, something inside me was relieved as I sat and answered questions while men swarmed throughout my house finding more psilocybin mushrooms and drug paraphernalia than I even knew I had. They loaded everything into a couple large vans, put me in the back seat of a squad car, and took me into the city to be booked. That was when fear took over. The sense of relief I had felt earlier was dominated by the awareness that I was really in a lot of trouble. The officer who had led the raid—the one who did all the talking at my house—took me into a room that was way too bright. He had me sign a confession. I didn't resist or demand to have a lawyer. I was in shock. I knew there was going to be no way out. I just wanted it to be over. So I cooperated. At about 5:30 in the morning—as I was expecting to be tossed into a jail cell—the arresting officer walked me to the door, said I would be contacted about a court date, and let me walk out.

The air was relatively warm. The eastern sky was just getting light. Birds were chirping. I walked to a pay phone and called a friend to drive me home. I watched the sunrise as I waited for my ride. I decided not to go to work that day. I was exhausted. When I called into work and told what happened, my boss panicked. Out of concern for the company image, the boss fired me. I went to bed and slept most of the day.

On April 29th, I woke up and realized that my life was a mess. I set out on a mad scramble to get my affairs in order. But I wasn't accustomed to order. The orderly world was the one in which I didn't like myself. I didn't like the way I felt. I didn't like the way I looked. I didn't recognize my achievements, and I didn't see any hope for improvement. Order was what I was accustomed to squelching. But I knew that wasn't an option this time. I knew that I had to be different.

I went to my closet to find something respectable to wear. Before that day, I hadn't noticed that I didn't own any good clothes. I had nothing that someone might wear to a wedding, or to a funeral, or to a court appearance. I had a couple nice shirts and a couple nice pairs of pants that I'd received as Christmas presents. I dressed the best I could, but my only shoes were work boots and a pair of gray tennis shoes that I bought at a flea market.

On the way out the door, I grabbed a pen, a clipboard and some paper. I wasn't sure what I was going to do, but I was going to try to do it systematically. Driving into the city, I brainstormed. At every stop sign, I added something to my list of things to do. When I reached the city, my first stop was the Goodwill Store. I broke my only ten dollar bill buying a pair of wingtips for three bucks. They were a little bit too large. It felt like I was wearing clown shoes. But I also felt they looked better than my gray tennies.

My next stop was the county old-folks home. I thought that it would look good when I went to court if I were doing some volunteer work. I talked to a lady at the front desk and filled out a volunteer application. I could tell by the way she looked at me that she knew I wasn't right. She took the application from me and told me someone would call. But her tone of voice was clearly saying, "In a pig's eye."

The next stop on my list was the Veteran's Administration. I thought that they might have some legal aid available for vets who had trouble adjusting to the civilian community. I explained my predicament to the man at the counter. Like the lady at the old folks home, the man at the V.A. looked at me like I was a two-headed toad. He said, "No. We can't help you. You should probably go to the end of the hall. They help people like you."

This was great news. It was only the third stop on my list, and I'd already hit pay dirt. I practically skipped down the hallway until I got to the last door.

The rusty gears that ran my brain started grinding and spinning as I read the sign that informed me I was about to enter the county drug-and-alcohol-treatment center. That was not on my list. But it looked like a great angle. If I could show the judge documentation that said I'd gotten help for my drug problem, he or she might think I'd turned my life around. I might be able to get off the hook. So I sat down in a little room with an intake counselor and explained my predicament. The counselor was very patient with me. She spoke to me with respect. And she listened with respect as I practically begged her to do something that would keep me from going to prison.

After she heard me out, the counselor said, "We can't do anything about your legal matters right now. Our concern is to get you well." We talked for about an hour and a half. She helped me see that my problem was not with the court but with myself. The court business was not the cause of my problem but a consequence. She was able to help me see that it wasn't enough for me to pretend to change. I had to really change. She gave me a list of meetings where I would be welcome, and she set up a schedule of counseling and education. The treatment was an outpatient program, so she gave me some pointers to follow—things to keep me out of trouble—as I was waiting for my first appointment.

The last thing we talked about before I left was God. That made me squirm. I'd abandoned God years before. The church I grew up with introduced me to a God I didn't like. I told her I wasn't superstitious, and whatever we were going to do in this treatment business was going to have to be done without God. She told me to forget that old God. She said I should just try praying and let a new idea of God emerge. I said it was going to be a stretch. She said, "What have you got to lose? You haven't done very well running your life without God." So I told her I would give it some thought. I put the papers and brochures on my clipboard and went on my way.

I don't know what other stops I had planned that day. I stopped my frantic search. I drove to a friend's house and told her about getting busted. I told her about getting treatment for alcoholism. She wanted to help me feel better. She pulled out her pot and smoked a joint with me. It made me cry.

I went home and tried to pray. I felt stupid at first. Then I felt angry. I was saying my first prayers in fifteen years, and I wanted results. I wanted dramatic results. I wanted lightning bolts. I wanted relief. I wanted hope. And all I felt was alone. Yet all alone, I managed to resist the urge—the overwhelming urge—to drink. Within a week, the boss who fired me had reconsidered the situation, and I got my job back. By the time I had my first counseling session at the treatment center, I had been sober for several days. Gradually, I found that praying actually helped—even though my faith was slight and my understanding of God was nonexistent. Gradually, I found hope. And when I was finally brought before the court, some inconceivable, unbelievable influence acted upon the judge who gave me the lightest possible sentence for the charges that were filed.

So today is the anniversary of that first awkward prayer. Tomorrow celebrates the anniversary of my first full day without any mood altering substances. This is not something I think about very much. But it's important for me to remember.

The turning point I am celebrating is probably the single most important achievement of my life. It was certainly the most difficult. And it's interesting to note how it happened. It began with a need. I could not have survived if I'd kept on with the life I was living. That need generated a crisis. That was the Universe banging me over the head to wake me up. After the crisis, I had an intention. I followed that intention with a plan. The plan was flawed, but it corrected itself as I followed it. And as it corrected itself, I was led to God.

Nowadays, I still have problems. They're not as bad as the old ones. I've learned to like myself. I've made friends with my feelings. I recognize and celebrate my achievements. But things still happen—in my mind and in my heart and in my experience. Things happen that are beyond my control. Rather than following my old path and letting things crush my faith and make me want to hide, I can face life with intention. I can decide what has to change, and I can take action. I can't always know exactly what I have to do, but I can make a plan. I can follow the plan. And I can pray. God still doesn't send me lightning bolts, but I'm okay with that. It keeps me from having to put out fires. Instead of lightning bolts, God sends me insights and opportunities. God helps me amend and adjust my plans as I go. And when I'm open to trying new approaches to old problems, things have a way of turning out for the best. That's the way my life works. And so it is.

OH SAMSON, MY SAMSON

I grew up in a perfect neighborhood for kids. There were lots of us. Everyday when the weather was nice, we gathered outside for play. Play emerged on its own. Someone would get an idea that others found appealing, and without effort, a game would begin. We never examined the process. We were kids. But looking back, it seems it always began with the news.

We'd gather on the sunny side of Terri Littlewood's house and everyone who had something interesting would give a report. We'd share the experiences we'd had since we last saw each other. We kept track of who had pizza, who got new toys, who had a babysitter, and whether or not the babysitter was any fun. By our story telling, we knew each other's grandparents and cousins. We knew all about each other's family vacations and outings. And there was one family outing that we all had in common that always drew the same response.

When on a morning someone announced that he or she had been to the zoo the day before, everyone would ask, "Did you see Samson?" Of course, the question was based on a foregone conclusion. Nobody would go to the zoo without seeing Samson. Samson was our gorilla. We loved him. And we never tired of hearing about him.

The stories were always stretched. They had to be. Samson usually just lay around in his glass enclosure watching the humans. But when the stories reached the neighborhood, everyone always claimed to have seen him being uncharacteristically active and fierce. In the stories, I heard of Samson jumping up, grabbing the truck tire that hung as his swing and stretching it like a rubber band. I heard of him pounding his chest and charging the thick glass that separated him from his visitors. But in real life, I only saw him lie there. On a good day, he picked his nose. But we loved him just the same.

Samson was like a god to us. He was huge and powerful. One black knuckle of Samson's finger was the size of a child's fist. His chest was as big as the back of Grandpa's chair. His gaze was penetrating. And he made eye contact with everyone who stood before him long enough, which naturally included every child who was old enough to not be terrified. We all had a personal relationship with Samson. We'd all looked into his soul, and he into ours.

A couple years ago, I went to the Milwaukee public museum. Inside the front door is a large display. I can't tell you all of what is on it, but I will always remember one thing. As I approached the display, I saw a skeleton of a large primate. I read the plaque to see exactly what it was. But it wasn't a what; it was a whom. It was Samson, my Samson, passed on from his life as the king of the zoo and now mounted sans flesh, naked and hollow, still and lifeless, a sculpture of bone. I saw the hollow sockets that once held the eyes into which I'd gazed with awe, respect and love. It reminded me of walking into a medieval cathedral festooned with the dried up bones of saints and clerics. It was compelling and morbid. And I felt so very, very sad.

It's interesting that Samson should be on my mind. I'm having one of those spells of questioning my path. I'm wondering if I'm spending my life the right way. For two and a half years, I've stood up on Sunday mornings and shared the truth that is in my soul with those who would come to hear. The most chairs that have been filled on a Sunday were twenty-two, and that was the first week. One Sunday, I held church alone. Not a single person came to hear my message. The past two Sundays, only one woman has shown up. The first week that happened, I sat down with her and we shared ideas and prayed. The second time—yesterday—she told me she wanted church the way I usually do it, so I stood before her and delivered my entire lesson the same as I would if two hundred were sitting before me.

I held her gaze. I gauged the clarity and power of my words by her facial expressions. By those indications, I gave a powerful lesson. She affirmed that for me afterwards by telling me how much she appreciates the depth of the thoughts that I prepare.

Part of me—my ego I suppose—is struggling with the attendance numbers. It's difficult for me to understand why so few people want to be reminded on Sundays that they are perfect expressions of the Divine Creative Genius of God. I know people are interested in God. I know people are interested in spiritual things. I want to touch their hearts and minds with life-affirming messages. But my inner cynic thinks that people would rather cleave to the dried up bones of saints and clerics.

I share a concept of God that extends beyond the human imagination. It is all-inclusive, favoring no one over another but loving all peoples all of the time. My inner cynic thinks people want a god that is smaller than that. It thinks they want a Samson god that can be contained in a glass case, adored on an occasional outing and forgotten most of the time. But God isn't something that's just for Sunday mornings. God is fully present everywhere at all times. God is in the way we put on our socks, the way we look into each other's eyes, and the way we eat our lunches. God is fully present in every thought, every feeling and every experience we have. God is responding to us in the very way we respond to God. It's worth an hour on Sunday morning to get very clear about that. At least, it is to me.

When I think of Samson, I get a little bit jealous. He had a large and faithful following. He inspired awe by simply pushing one of his massive black fingers into a cavernous nostril. On the other hand, he spent his life in confinement, and I am free. I can do whatever I want. So I guess that explains why I keep getting up on Sundays and sharing my message—even if only one chair is filled.

Yesterday morning, my congregation was small—but I had a 100-percent approval rating. By that fact, I have to say that church was a smashing success. Right now, my life doesn't look exactly the way I want it to, but at least I'm doing what I love to do. I don't think Samson could have said that. So rather than worrying about what the other churches are doing, rather than worrying about whose bones are on display where, I guess I'll just celebrate the things I have. I have years of good memories. I have the future ahead of me. I have a spiritual practice that satisfies my needs.

What fun. And so it is.

I GOT STUFF

I got stuff—you got stuff—all God's childrens got stuff
When I get to heaven gonna take off my stuff
I'm gonna mend all over God's heaven, heaven
Everybody talkin' 'bout heaven ain't a-goin' there heaven, heaven
I'm gonna mend all over God's heaven

I know the vast Universe is filled with things that are inspiring. The Universe is whole, perfect and complete. I could remind you of the awesome, peaceful magnificence of a rainbow or a summer sunset. I could praise the miracles of childhood innocence or the beauty of friendship and love. But all you'd get from that is a watered-down dose of things you already know. Meanwhile, homeless people would still be begging for spare change. Children across the planet would still be starving at a rate of about one every three seconds. And lonely people everywhere could trip me up with the question, "If God is so wonderful, why does my heart feel like it is breaking?"

Here's the deal: homeless people beg, children starve and hearts break, and it's all because of imbalance. God is in balance, but God possesses infinite possibilities. Among the infinite possibilities of God is the possibility of imbalance. All people are children of God; therefore, we have all inherited the qualities inherent to God. And a quality we seem to express as humans—among the infinity of possibilities—is imbalance.

Imbalance is not what we have come here to express. We are here to enjoy abundant life, freedom and love. But somehow along the way, we accumulate stuff. That stuff throws us out of balance. The way back to balance is the elimination of stuff.

A few weeks ago, I made a decision to eliminate some of my stuff. Decision is a powerful force. The Universe responded by shedding light upon my biggest stuff piles, and I started to shovel away. But some stuff piles are not easy to find. And when we do find them, we discover there is a more significant stuff pile underneath. This weekend, the Universe led me to a significant stuff pile. I'm dying to share.

On Saturday night, I went to my thirty-year high school reunion. Hoo, Baby! I found some stuff there.

I arrived early. It began as an awkwardly pleasant gathering. I saw people whom I hadn't seen in ten years. I exchanged a little small talk—an activity at which I tend to suck. And it was complicated in this particular gathering by the fact that I was somewhat of a loner in high school. When I sat in English class or algebra (twice) or German (didn't learn a thing) or history (hated it), I took on the mantle of class clown, but after school when friends gathered for extra-curricular activities, I went my own way. People knew me, but very few knew me in any meaningful way—just as I did not know them.

My discomfort soon faded as people from my grade school started to arrive. These were people whom I had known since fourth grade. I felt a special bond to them, and I was sincerely happy to see them. Among our grade-school group of about a dozen people, there were three girls—excuse me, women—upon whom I had preadolescent crushes. There were boys—oops, men—with whom I'd wrestled in the grass beside the playground. We had all sung together in Christmas pageants, decorated bulletin boards, gone on field trips and danced in gym class. We learned together that JFK had been shot. We all caught Beatle-mania together. These were my family of sorts, and although I didn't tell them I loved them, my heart was singing and my soul was dancing just to be in their midst.

When the reunion moved from the lobby/bar to the dining room, a cluster of us from my grade school took a table together. It was weird in that it wasn't weird. It felt perfectly natural to be sitting among these people. I couldn't feel any differences wrought by years of different experiences. I simply felt I was among my friends. Naturally, we talked a little about our careers and achievements. The people with families passed around pictures of their children. We talked a little about travel and interests. And we reminisced. That's when my stuff started coming up.

Six of the people at my table had been in my fourth grade class. I've written about fourth grade before. That was the year my life went to hell. By some seemingly cruel trick of the Universe, I was accelerated from second grade right into fourth. I never adjusted academically or socially, and for years I've been processing—realizing the reasons for my nagging sense of loneliness, identifying the roots of my years of alcoholism and drug addictions and tracing the source of years of low self-esteem. Through countless hours of prayer, meditation, affirmations, and forgiveness work, I've managed to transcend the damage and come to peace with my past. At least, that was what I thought. I thought I'd shoveled up that stuff pile pretty well.

But the Universe has an infinity of tricks up Its sleeve. And I made a decision to eliminate stuff. Knock and the door will open.

As we sat around the dinner table, we recalled the names of our teachers and what they were all like. One of the girls—excuse me, women—said, "Eeww. Do you remember fourth grade?"

And another one said, "Eeww, yeah. The bad-boy class." And they began talking about specific individuals—boys I remember to be bullies.

As I listened to what they were saying, I almost choked on my heart. I swallowed it back down, turned to the woman next to me and said, "Wait a minute. Explain this to me. Bad-boy class?" She told me it was true. Among the educational experiments they were pulling back then, somebody got the brilliant idea that if all of the most disruptive boys from the third grade were placed in the same class, only one teacher would have to deal with them. Perhaps there was some sort of notion of uniformity in dispensing discipline? It was mainly a crazy idea, and the way it was explained to me, all of the girls in the class suffered. The woman who was explaining it to me said she never wanted to go to school. She used to look up diseases in the encyclopedia, and when she woke up in the morning, she would tell her mother she was ill. She'd describe the symptoms and offer a diagnosis. She came up with diseases her mother had never heard of. Her mother was a teacher at another school, and she eventually figured out what the problem was. She would call the school administrators and try to explain that they couldn't keep all the most poorly behaved boys in the same class. But the administrators didn't listen.

I remembered feigning illnesses to stay home too, but I did not know I was in the bad boy class. I was eight years old. I was trying to learn how to act as if I were nine. I did so by observing the boys around me. And I learned that to be more mature I had to be sassy, unruly and destructive. I couldn't compete academically because I didn't have the advantage of a year of third grade. I couldn't compete physically because a child's body only grows as fast as it wants to. So to rise up to the stature of my peers, I tried to learn to be crude, sneaky and mean. Swearing and lying were easy pick up. Being mean was a little more difficult. It required a certain toughness that I didn't have. I tried to compensate by assuming the behaviors of tough kids. I started smoking before I got to junior high. I started drinking as soon as I figured out how to steal liquor from my parents. I shunned all homework. I shoplifted and vandalized. I picked on kids who were smaller than me—those who were two grades or more behind me—yet I still retained the consciousness of a victim. All the way through school, I was a magnet for bullies. I could not act tough enough to make the genuine tough kids believe it.

The woman who explained the fourth-grade-class dynamics was not fooled by my attempts to be one of the bad boys. She said she always felt sad for me because she could see how I was struggling. She knew I was a good boy. She knew something I did not know. In that class with all the loose cannons, the teacher had her hands full. She didn't have time to give me the attention I needed. She made the bad boys stay after school to punish them. She made me stay after school to complete my work. In my eight-year-old mind, that meant I was one of them.

I did not spend my class reunion thinking about all these things. I really enjoyed the evening. Most of the people who were there have done quite well. In my heart, I celebrated their successes—even as a part of me felt a little jealous. Jealousy is a bad seed. I pushed it out of my mind. We all had some laughs. My grade-school friends and I had a group photo taken. But then it was time to leave. I had to prepare for church in the morning.

When I got out to my truck, I had to sit for a while. I had tears in my eyes. I was feeling the joy that surpasses understanding. I felt a deep soul connection to the friends from fourth grade with whom I broke bread. None of the bullies were at the reunion. The people at the reunion were the kids that I should have been modeling myself after. But even among the distractions of the bad boys, we had bonded in that special way that children do. We were together before our lives were complicated by sexual tension. We played together before our lives were thrown out of balance by accumulated piles of stuff. The love I felt as I waited for my tears to clear was pure and beautiful and the way I wish I could feel for all people. It felt mystical. Then I drove home.

It's amazing how much thinking a person can do in a half-hour drive. By the time I got home, the beauty of seeing old friends was shattered by the anger of new information about old issues. By the time I walked into my house, I was pissed, and I couldn't sleep for hours as I calculated the millions for which I would sue if there were any justice in life. I compared my life to the lives of my childhood friends. I put price tags on all of the things I don't have, and I blamed my every lack and loss of family, friends and income on the school administrators that I thought I'd forgiven years ago.

Now, a few days and a lot of thought later, I get to put myself back together. Now, I get to remind myself—over and over until I get it—that every soul has a purpose. My soul's purpose was not to have any easy, direct path to a wife and children in a big new home in the suburbs. My soul's purpose was not to climb a corporate ladder or build a business empire. My soul's path has led me to ministry. I arrived here by a long, circuitous, painful route. If things had been too easy, I might not have turned to the spiritual life. Or else I would not be able to speak with authority about overcoming hardship.

The spiritual work that I must now do is exactly the same as the spiritual work I've been doing and teaching for years. I must first accept responsibility for my thoughts, for my feelings and for the conditions of my life. I must accept the fact that all of creation looks exactly as it does as a result of everything that has come before. I must face my life and know that no amount of anger or resentment is going to change the past. I must forgive. I do this by reminding myself—as many times as necessary—that the things of life are just stuff. The essence of life is God. God is peace. God is love. God is joy. God is beauty. God is fully present everywhere at all times, so the gifts of peace, love, joy and beauty are always available to me. They are my birthright. I cannot access them when I'm angry. I cannot access them when I compare myself to others.

As I sat at the reunion celebrating life with my friends, we really only shared the best parts. We didn't have time to go deep and talk about the things that trouble our hearts. But if we had, we would have probably found we are all very much the same. Life exists in grand abundance for one and all, but it is filled with trade-offs. It is a balance of pain and pleasure. The people whom I admired (with my secret whit of jealousy) for their responsible positions and financial successes probably had a little voice inside them yearning for the ease and simplicity of my life. The people whom I admired (with just a hint of envy) for their spouses and children probably had an eye on my freedom to come and go as I please and on the fact that I don't have to pay anyone's college tuition. I have a life that is quiet and contemplative. It is the life that suits my soul. My soul created it by teaching me at an early age to be alone. It's not bad. It gives me time to think and sort. And as I think and sort, something important is sure to be revealed.

Somewhere among all my piles of stuff is a nugget of wisdom. I'm not sure what it is, but I'm here to share it with the world. It may not house the homeless. It may not be the answer to world hunger. It may not heal broken hearts. But on the other hand, it may do all those things. I'm determined to find out. All I have to do is get my life into balance. I do that by clearing away my stuff. And I find the stuff I need to clear as the Universe reveals it to me. Thank you, God. And so it is.

SACRIFICE

"Sacrifice" is a scary word. It conjures images of cruel and primitive rituals. It suggests throwing away things that one loves. If you ask a room full of people how the word makes them feel, most will say they don't like it. But it's a good thing most of the time.

I'm not saying I endorse slaughtering farm animals or virgins (or virgin farm animals). I'm just saying that life is full of trade offs. And often we sacrifice things we love for the sake of things we love even more. Think of the people who sacrifice their freedom for families, or their weekends to help others. The things people sacrifice are precious, but the rewards of making honorable and courageous sacrifices can be great. The rewards can last a long, long time.

This past weekend, I saw a few childhood friends, life-long friends, with whom I haven't connected in a meaningful way for many years. Sixteen years ago, one of them moved to Amsterdam. The other one has been around, but during all those years my relationship with him was thrown off balance by political postures. For a while, he was my boss. After that, I became the traitor who left and took a large business account with me. Gradually, I became his customer. Our relationship went from me serving him to a silent possibility of animosity to him serving me. During all those years, an artificial tension strained all our interactions.

Recently, the friend with whom relations were strained made a business move that ended our professional relationship. This eliminated the barrier that separated us, but we were in the old habit of avoiding casual contact. Then our other friend—the one from Amsterdam—announced he was coming to town. He invited us both—the alienated old friends—to a family gathering on Pewaukee Lake. It was the first time I'd seen him in years. And it was even longer since I was able to greet the friend-become-business-acquaintance at eye-level, as equals, as old friends.

When we were boys, the three of us rode bikes and threw stones together. As we started stumbling awkwardly into our teens, we shared a cache of nudist magazines. As we developed in adolescent stealth, we started sneaking booze from our parents—snitching about a shot from each of the bottles in the liquor cabinet and pouring it all together in mason jars. We were too stupid to sweeten the mixture with fruit juice or soda. We would camp out in the back yard and get smashed sipping our vulgar concoctions until we barfed in the nearby field and crawled back to our sleeping bags to pass out.

When we were old enough to drive, we learned of bars on Pewaukee Lake that didn't check ID cards. We'd drive out to the lake on the weekends and swagger pimply-faced up to the bar for fifteen-cent tap beers. I always drank too many. Somebody else always drove home.

The summer when I was seventeen, I discovered marijuana. I loved it. It made me forget my teen angst, and for a little while, everything made me laugh. I shared my discovery with the friend who would later move to Amsterdam. He loved it too, and he told our other friend—the one for whom I would someday work—whose family owned a cottage on Pewaukee Lake.

One Friday evening in July or August, my friends called me. Mr. Amsterdam had purchased a bag of weed, so Mr. Lake Cottage could try it. They asked me to come along. In 1972, I was incapable of saying, "No" to pot. So we piled into my car and drove out to the lake cottage. At dark, we climbed into the motorboat and drove to the middle of the lake. We shut it down and as we rocked in the dark water, started to smoke. It could have been a wonderful evening. It could have.

Gentle waves lapped the sides of the creaking boat as the pungent aroma of smoldering cannabis hung in the warm evening air. We were right at that point when the effects should be kicking in when the red lights and siren of a police launch split the night at our stern. For a moment we panicked. In an instant, Mr. Lake Cottage started the motor and began to flee. Mr. Amsterdam said, "Throw out the dope. Throw out the dope." I'm not even sure who threw it, but the sealed sandwich bag made an arc through the beam of the searchlight and floated conveniently in the path of the police-boat. Meanwhile, Mr. Lake Cottage realized there was nowhere to run and shut down our engine. We waited.

The police fished our stash from the surface of the lake, and then they pulled alongside. They told us they were only going to give us a ticket for not having our lights on until we gave them our pot and tried to flee.

When they determined we were just three clean-cut, pimply minors, they escorted us back to the lake cottage. My friend's parents were not there. They would be soon, but we didn't say so. The police lined us up on the pier. We stood looking down at about the policemen's' knees. They told us all to tell our parents to expect a phone call in the morning. Then one of them said, "Before we go, does anybody want to claim this?" He held out the bag of pot and let it swing in front of us. In the awkward silence, I suddenly felt responsible. I was the oldest. I was the first one of us to try pot. I was the bad influence.

Among the three of us, I was the one who had a history of being in trouble. My parents were the ones who had gotten calls from the police before—for my vandalism and underage drinking. My sense of responsibility was suddenly bolstered by courage. I suddenly saw an opportunity to do something courageous. With my eyes still cast downward, I said, "It's mine. They didn't know I had it with me. I threw it when I got scared."

The three of us waited at the cottage for the first set of parents to get the news. When they arrived, I repeated my story. "It's mine. They didn't know I had it with me. I threw it when I got scared." That was what my friend's parents needed to hear. They never questioned my story. They needed their son to be innocent. They told me I was never welcome there again. My other friend's father wasn't fooled. He knew we were all in on it. But my story held up, and I was the only one to be called into court.

That in itself was a happy ending, but last Friday night, I stood once again on the dark shore of the same lake. We looked at the water and remembered. My friends told me that they had always been grateful that I'd make that sacrifice. But for years, they also lived with the regret that they let me do it. For years, they wished they had spoken up when I did and said, "No. It's ours. We're all in on it." They lived with a feeling that they had let me down.

I never felt they let me down. I never regretted the gift of myself that I had given for them. They were my friends. And thirty years after our brush with the law, I hugged them both and tried to explain that I'd made that sacrifice as much for myself as for them. They struggled to understand. I struggled to explain. I was a seventeen-year-old kid with a bad reputation and nothing to be proud of. I suddenly saw an opportunity to do something honorable. And while publicly there wasn't any glory in it, in my heart I'd done something that I could feel proud of.

I'm not sure my friends understood. I think sacrifices are that way. They are usually things of great honor and little glory—things like keeping commitments even when more attractive opportunities come along, things like raising children, things like giving gifts of service that may never be fully appreciated or understood.

There is something I did not understand as I stood on the pier and spoke those words that I knew would infuriate my parents and cost me some freedom. I did not understand that God is all there is. I hadn't yet come to understand that God is infinite, and infinity by definition cannot be divided. I did not yet know that all I can see, or hear, or touch, or know—or even imagine—is imbued with the Omnipresent Spirit from which all Creation arises. As I stood on the pier and made my sacrifice, I was offering myself to God—I was offering myself to God expressing as my friends and their parents. Years would pass before I would understand that any gift of service is a gift to God, and by a Law of Reciprocity, God gives equal or greater gifts in return. For the months that followed the floating-marijuana caper, I was grounded from going anywhere but to work. I was on probation until my eighteenth birthday. And I lived those days with great respect for myself. I learned I was strong enough to make a sacrifice for a friend. And I have never regretted what happened.

So that is what I'm remembering now as I approach new opportunities to make new sacrifices. The inner rewards are far greater than outer appearances will reveal. And the biggest part of life is what happens in our hearts. And so it is.

Scott de Snoo

FINDING LOVE

Tonight I'm thinking about ruts—because I'm not in one. I'm thinking about change. And I'm thinking about the nature of reality. And I'm thinking about lots of other things as well—because I have fallen in love.

In the span of a few short weeks, my whole Universe appears to have changed. And yet, it hasn't changed at all. I've simply opened myself to perceiving it better and receiving it better. I've changed. And it feels like a surprise to me, but it really shouldn't.

A few years ago, I started writing spiritual stories and lessons from my life that I called "musings" and sending them out to an email list. I did it to get out of a rut. I felt lonely and isolated. I'd felt that way for most of my life. Even in a crowd, I felt separate and misunderstood. And from that lonesome place, I decided to reach out. I decided to make connections, and to make those connections meaningful by opening my heart and revealing my innermost self to the world. I shared my fears. I shared my pain. I revealed things of which I was ashamed. I also revealed the things that gave me joy, but the things to which most people responded were the darkest spots on my journey.

I think that by sharing the darkness, I helped people escape the same sense of isolation that I was trying to overcome. It helped people see that we all share a similar range and depth of emotion. We are never really as alone as we may feel. And the process of sharing produced the effects I was after. This process of sharing made me more willing to be vulnerable. It also made me more able to recognize the pain that others feel. It helped me grow to be more compassionate. It opened my heart to a greater experience of love. Yet it didn't seem to be leading to the thing I desired most. My connections were growing and deepening, but I was still without a special person with whom to share my life's journey. I had much love in my life, but I wasn't "in love."

I did have a few false starts. I made a few friends with whom I tried going through the motions of a relationship. But the beauty and depth of a genuine romantic union were not fully present. I felt that I was trapped in an endless rut—going forward, but still not free.

It reminds me of a story I heard a few years ago. It was about a man who lived in the desert. He had a camel, and he had a well. He had little else. It was the desert. He could have ridden his camel out of the desert, but he didn't know how he would do it and survive. He was afraid to go too far from his well. He prayed for a better life, but he stayed right where he was. One day, his camel fell down the well. He knew he couldn't drink from a well that was contaminated with a camel, and he suddenly realized he had nothing. He knew he must move. But before he ventured into the desert, he felt he should cover the well. That way, his camel would have a proper burial, and future passersby wouldn't be at risk of drinking from a contaminated well. So the man started pouring pails of sand down the well. As the sand accumulated on the camel's back, the camel grew annoyed and shook it off into the water where he stood. Soon, the camel was up to his knees in sandy muck. So the camel pulled his big, flat feet out of the muck and stepped up onto it. The sand kept coming down. The camel kept shaking it off. And each time the camel was buried to his knees, he pulled his big, flat feet out of the sand and stepped up onto it. And in a few hours, the well was almost full, and the camel simply stepped out of it. Then the man had a camel but no well, so he climbed onto the camel's back to ride out of the desert and into the better life he had prayed for.

That reveals the nature of reality. There is always something greater happening than what we can see.

From this chair in which I am sitting, I've been piling in the sand—not even fully aware of the effects I've been producing. The well was the isolation with which I'd lived so long that I was afraid to walk away from it. My camel was the lonely consciousness that I wanted to overcome. The flow of words each Monday night was the sand that was supposed to cover it over. But what I succeeded in doing was to fill the isolation, which elevated my consciousness and now allows me to step freely into a whole new experience—without the isolation.

I can't begin to describe the joy. And the story—the real story—is a lesson in itself. One of the readers of the spiritual musings that I send to my email list is a woman whom I see a few times a year. Our friendship has grown gradually, gently, and genuinely. She wasn't trying to win my heart. For the first year of our friendship, she thought I was gay. After I revealed I was not, a slight element of flirtatiousness entered our interactions, but I didn't think anything of it. I flirt with women all the time—at least I used to.

A few weeks ago, she and I spent another of our infrequent weeks together. We flirted a little more than ever before. But we talked about it. We live far away from each other. A relationship would be totally impractical. We agreed that we had genuine affection for each other, but we expressed it in a very careful, reserved, and noncommittal way. At least that's what we thought we were doing.

Within a few days of returning to my home, I realized that I missed her terribly. My weekly exercise of writing the musings had gotten me into the habit of freely sharing my feelings. I sent her an email and told her what was happening in my heart. And she responded that the same thing was happening in hers. We'd fallen in love.

Now one week later—after exchanging forty-eight emails and at least ten long phone calls—we've fallen even deeper. We both agree we've fallen more deeply than either of us ever has before. Now here's the funny part. When people fall in love, they naturally want to tell the whole world. She has been sharing the news with some of our closest mutual friends—other people who are around during our infrequent weeks together. And while she expects our friends to get as excited as we are and jump up and down laughing giddily, they just calmly look at her and say, "This is supposed to be news?"

We were the last to know! And this reveals something wonderful about the nature of reality. It reveals the nature of creation. All things begin gradually, and the creative process of the Universe is at work long before we ever see results. As my love and I knew our lives as separate and lonely entities, the Universe was preparing us for the moment when we would be ready to perceive and receive the truth. Our more perceptive friends could see it, but they knew they couldn't interfere with our process.

I share this because I know that life often feels like a rut. When I was working my way through college, it seemed endless. Then suddenly, I was a graduate. I've had jobs that felt like a life sentence of misery. Then suddenly, a new opportunity appeared. As I've gone through this process of opening my heart, I've told many people that I was discouraged by the absence of apparent results. They offered me encouragement. They told me the right one was going to come along. They told me I was a good catch, and the one I was seeking was worth the wait. I had trouble believing. I felt like I was in a rut. Now suddenly, I see they were right. Suddenly, I know they saw something happening to me that I couldn't see for myself. And now I clearly see that all of the wonderful surprises that seem to come suddenly are really the things we are gradually preparing ourselves to receive.

So my invitation to you is one of hope. We all have aspects of our lives that we are working to change. And we all go through periods when it seems the change will never come. We all feel discouragement sometimes. But if you've chosen a path, and you've been following it consistently, something is happening. Something is changing.

The nature of reality is two-fold. There is the seen, and there is the unseen. The unseen comes first. And It is always at work. It is changing your life right now. And It is probably trying to offer you assurance. Stay alert. You don't have to be the last to know. When your friends offer you words of encouragement, don't shrug them off. Don't think they are only trying to make you feel better. Just as the Universe is preparing all the aspects of your life to lift you to your next goal, It is giving you the words you need to hear through the voices of your friends. The Universe works this way because It is wonderful—and so are you. And so it is.

Scott de Snoo

LOVE AND LAW

I'm looking at a bear. He's a little panda—only 10" tall not counting his ears. I'm not sure how old he is. He might be older than me. All I know is that I've known him as long as I can remember.

He slept with me when I was a little boy. He played with me a lot too. When I inspect him closely, I can see that most of his seams were hand-repaired by my mother. Both his arms have been reattached as well as his head. The stitches up the middle of his back are not original. The seams that separate the dingy white middle of his face from the black sides have been redone. The fur is worn off the front of his nose, and the bare fabric beneath must have been worn through on one side because the black fabric is stretched way over toward the middle leaving his face slightly askew. His parts that once were white are the same dull brownish-gray as the stuffing that protrudes from the couches of college students. In all his worn and dirty glory, he lives in my home as a reminder. He is a testament to love.

Once when I was a very small boy, I was getting ready for bed on a summer evening. I had my pajamas on. My mom helped me brush my teeth. She opened my bed, and I was ready to crawl in when I realized my bear was gone. I don't remember crying, but I'm sure I did. My parents interrogated me and determined the last place I had my bear was in the back yard by the swing set. I remember watching through the dark out the window as my father lit matches—one after the other—taking advantage of the brief initial blaze of the sulphur tips until he spotted my bear lying on the lawn. He brought it in to me, and I slept.

I was 18 the year my father died. The drinking age in Wisconsin was 18 then. This was a bad combination of influences for me. I did not know how to deal with the grief and the fear of living without the safety cushion of having a dad. I couldn't stay sober. It was too painful for me.

I worked for two kind men who were deeply disturbed by the way I was living my life. When I ambled into work late smelling of alcohol, they scolded me. I gave them ample reason to fire me. But they both had sons who were near my age. They could see my pain. They tried to lift me out of it.

One Sunday, I was with a few friends—the kind of friends you attract when all you do is drink. It was the middle of the day. We had just finished drinking up everything in the house, and we thought it would be a good idea to walk downtown and drink some more. We didn't get four blocks before one of my friends started barfing on the sidewalk. A squad car pulled over and two policemen confronted us. I got defensive and belligerent. The police told the friend who wasn't sick to go home. They took the barfer and me to the courthouse to sober up. We came to and demanded to be released at about two o'clock on Monday morning. By the time I got home, slept a little, got cleaned up, and got to the warehouse, I was late for work again.

One of my bosses confronted me, but I thought that for a change it wasn't my fault. For a change, I did not smell like alcohol. I took credit for that. And I didn't feel it was fair that I should have been locked up. I felt that walking down the street was a responsible thing to do because it meant I was not driving drunk. I tried to explain my point of view, but my boss stopped me and told me that cities had laws prohibiting public drunkenness. I said, "Well, I didn't know."

My boss said, "Ignorance of the law is no excuse."

From that day forward, my boss put me on probation, and I actually quit drinking for a few months.

The Law of Creation is a simple one. Everything we are is a prayer, and every prayer is answered.

I've been thinking about what it means to live a spiritually directed life. If we want a fulfilling experience, it's not enough to believe in God. Most people believe in God, and fulfillment eludes most people. This is because most people separate their spiritual life from their physical life. They think it's enough to show up for church on Easter and Christmas and to say, "Thank you God" before the Thanksgiving meal. Then they go back to struggling with life the rest of the year. But God doesn't give a rip snort about Christmas, Easter and Thanksgiving. Those are just punctuation marks in our human experience. God is on duty all the time. God listens and responds to every whisper of our hearts.

And God's only response is, "Yes." It's the Law.

If we walk around believing that life is a shit sandwich and every day we take a bite, God says, "Yes." If we believe that work is tedious and the world is out to get us, God says, "Yes." If we believe that love is an illusion, and relationships are difficult, God says, "Yes." We can go to church on Sundays and declare to the corners of the Universe that our lives are filled with abundance, but if we spend the rest of our time believing that we are getting cheated and worrying we're going to come up short before the next paycheck, God hears our beliefs far more loudly than the prayers we say on Sunday. And God always says, "Yes."

The Law of Creation is simple. Living in harmony with it is not easy. Part of the problem is ignorance. People just don't realize that everything they think, do or say is a prayer. Many spiritual masters have tried to explain it. All the sacred texts of the world urge readers to keep their hearts pure. They all emphasize right thinking and right action. They were all written by people who understood the Law of Creation. They were all written by people who wanted to give readers the understanding they needed to consistently produce fulfilling experiences. But people don't learn well. Some teachers just gave up. Moses got tired of trying to explain Spiritual Law. He finally resorted to writing commandments—rules to follow that would at least keep people's behavior appropriate long enough for them to perhaps see the benefit. But changing behavior isn't even enough.

Changing behavior is like trying to bargain with God. It's like saying, "I'll be good if you go outside and get my bear." But God is not fooled. God knows our motives. God knows our beliefs.

When my father went outside with a book of matches and found my bear in the dark, it was an act of great love. When I received my bear, it was a gift of grace. But grace befalls the innocent, not the ignorant. When I was arrested for public drunkenness, I was ignorant—I was ignoring the obvious to suit my own purposes. I grew up in a civilized and loving home. I went to Sunday school and learned the 10 Commandments. I knew right from wrong, but I tried to alter the rules with which I'd been raised.

Sometimes, we experience the illusion of grace. We stray from our spiritual principles, and we get away with it. The Sunday I was arrested was not the first time I walked down Grand Avenue drunk. I did it enough times that I started thinking it was okay. But when we do things that do not serve our highest good and the highest good of the Universe, all of the power of God shifts to coordinate exactly the right series of space-time events to create an appropriate response. Sometimes, the coordination takes a little while. God has an infinity of other space-time events with which the new one must harmonize. The time it takes to bring the creative process together is not grace. It's just time. One might try to anticipate how God is using time. One might try to understand all that God must do to create the next gift—or the next painful lesson—but that would be trying to understand infinity. We're not equipped to do that.

So the best we can do is to monitor our thoughts. The best we can do is to truly live a spiritual life. And we can begin by remembering it is a full-time job. It extends into every area and every moment of our lives. It takes training and discipline. It requires that we keep our hearts and minds free of judgments, resentments and fears. It requires that we let go of beliefs in lack, limitation and disease. And when we slip back into old patterns of struggle, it requires that we remember that getting away with it is not grace. God is listening with absolute Love, and God is responding by absolute Law.

I invite you to remember the Power and Presence. I invite you to recognize there is a sacred connection between everything you are and everything you experience. God is on purpose. God is responding to you. And God loves you—because you are wonderful. And so it is.

LOVING SERVICE

The past seven weeks, as I've been floating through life with my feet barely touching the floor, I've been observing what makes each moment special. I've been listening to the things that make my heart sing. And I recognize that the spiritual practice of being in love is a model of how I relate to the world, even as the spiritual practice of relating to the world is a model for being in love. And I'm delighted to discover that I'm good at it.

I spent many years yearning. I had many false starts. I was beginning to think that I lacked some unimaginable skills that everyone else seems to possess. It was difficult and painful to come home each evening to my books and my weights and a bowl of cereal for supper. So I studied the way of love. I read that to attract love into my life, I must always be loving. I learned of the spiritual practice of selfless service, and I applied it in every opportunity I could find.

In our society, especially in the 1980s and '90s, there was a toxic prevailing attitude of selfishness. They were times of conspicuous consumption and rapid advancement. People were infected by the question, "What's in it for me?" Fortunes were made and celebrated on TV and in magazines. Yet all around me, I saw people's hearts breaking as they failed to keep up. I saw people's spirits breaking as their greatest efforts went unrecognized, and they were passed up for promotions or downsized out of their careers.

I had the infection. I wanted the big jackpot, the big house and the new cars. I tried multi-level marketing schemes and stuffed envelopes at home with bullshit offers promising great rewards for stuffing envelopes at home. I bought lottery tickets. I bought magazines and entered the Publishers Clearinghouse Sweepstakes. My hunger for riches is even what attracted me to New Thought, a spiritual teaching derived from the works of great mystics like Ernest Holmes, who tell us that we are responsible for our reality. When I happened—almost by accident—into a Sunday-morning service and heard that I could create the life I desired by using the creative power of my mind, I thought I'd found my pot of gold. And indeed, using the principles of scientific prayer, my income did increase. The circumstances of my life did improve dramatically. But I still felt unfulfilled.

As I studied New Thought, a deeper awareness emerged. I began to recognize that fulfillment was not something that could be measured in dollars. I began having little experiences that revealed my greatest joy came when I was attuned to the natural cycles of life and aware of the sanctity of all creation. I realized that the thing I needed more than money was a deeper sense of the sacred. So I expanded my spiritual base by spending evenings in meditation with the Buddhists.

I continued studying New Thought. I continued practicing scientific prayer. But I also took a few evenings a week to stop striving. On my Zen nights, I quit trying to apply the creative power of my mind and simply sat in silence, surrendering my mind to the whispers of the Divine mystery. I gradually began to recognize that there was a shift occurring all around me. Other people besides myself were growing weary of the accumulation model of life. They were seeking greater meaning, and the bookshelves that were formerly filled with the success-seekers' guides to power handshakes, dressing for success, and networking with the sharks were suddenly displaying books about slowing down, living simply, and finding peace in feeling grateful.

One evening at the Zen group, the abbot gave a short dharma talk. He explained the value of selfless service as a spiritual practice. He said that the happiest people were those who approached their work by not asking, "What's in it for me?" but by asking, "How can I serve?"

The next morning, and for many mornings thereafter, I drove to work with the car radio off. As I drove, I chanted softly. Over and over, I asked myself, "How can I serve?" And everything in my experience changed. The workplace was transformed from a place of stressful contention to an arena in which to practice compassion and loving kindness. I recognized that everyone there could benefit from my services—both the services that were in my job description and the service of relieving their suffering with gentle words and small acts of kindness. My work became my spiritual practice. I thought I was some sort of guru. I thought I had discovered something entirely new. The truth was that I'd known it all along.

As I now enjoy my new spiritual practice of being in love, my sweetheart and I spend a lot of time sharing our histories. The other night, we were talking about the things people do to make living together meaningful even after the initial excitement has faded. I heard myself reminiscing about my grandparents. They were in love. They'd lived together a long time. Observing them as a child, I assumed that they'd been together an eternity. My grandfather was retired. I don't think my grandmother ever had a job. But they were both busy, active people. They had the oldest house on the block with the biggest yard, the longest driveway, the largest garden, and the most buildings. They had to do a lot of maintenance to keep it nice, which they did.

The detail I recalled the other night was that they both identified their chores as service to each other. When I went to their house hoping to be entertained, my grandmother would tell me things like, "I have to cook Grandpa's supper," or "I have to finish washing the floor for Grandpa." Similarly, my grandfather would say things like, "I have to hoe Grandma's garden," or "I have to wash the car for Grandma."

It was a wonderful memory to have after all these years. I never heard either of my grandparents complain about the work they had to do. Neither ever thought of what rewards they expected or desired for the things they did. The rewards were intrinsic because they were in service. The chores they did were gifts of love. Their lives together were a spiritual practice, and they were fulfilled. And they stayed in love—even when they were as old as the hills, which is they way they looked to me.

I doubt that my grandparents consciously designed their life as a Zen practice. I doubt they even knew the word Zen. And their understanding of Buddhism was probably gleaned from watching Yul Brynner in "The King and I" on "Saturday Night at the Movies." But the beauty of spiritual practice is that you don't have to understand it. It's enough just to do it. The rewards are the same.

Funny things happened after I started the practice of chanting, "How can I serve." Of course, the obvious happened. I stopped resenting my job, and that was good. But what I found even more rewarding was that people started really liking me—and trusting me—and they would come to me to talk about their most personal problems because they knew I was their friend. But the most interesting change occurred on my paycheck. As if by magic, my income suddenly started taking great leaps. I got unexpected raises. I got unexpected bonuses. All of the prayers I had done for greater income were suddenly answered when I stopped looking for the answer and lived my life in loving service.

Now after several years of living a life of loving service, my greatest prayer of all has been answered. Living from a place of love has attracted love to me. I still haven't fully adjusted to the contentment that replaced the yearning that I used to feel. I still haven't fully adjusted to the fact that I can hear the one I love say, "I love you" ten or twenty times a day. And actually, I hope I never adjust to it. I hope it still feels this startlingly new when I'm as old as the hills. And there is a good chance it will. As I remember to treasure my love with gifts of service, my love will grow deeper, which will remind me to treasure my love with gifts of service, and my love will grow deeper . . .. Such is the way of love.

God is all there is. God is everywhere and in everything. Therefore, any gift is a gift to God. Any gift is a gift from God. Any gift of service is God giving to Itself. So to participate in the eternal flow of God's loving energy, we need only open our hearts to giving and receiving. That is spiritual practice. And whether or not we understand it, we still enjoy the rewards—because we are wonderful. And so it is.

PERFECTIONISM

Right now, the woman of my dreams is driving a diesel truck up the interstate with two big dogs beside her on the seat. She's pulling a flatbed trailer that's carrying her '66 Buick Wildcat, and she's singing along to oldies on the radio.

It sounds like a country-western song, but I'm not making it up. The woman of my dreams really is coming to live with me, and all that stuff about the truck is true. It holds a good lesson in the nature of perfection.

A few years ago, I got serious about finding my perfect partner. I listed all of the qualities I wanted her to have. Then I went through the list and made sure that I possessed all of the qualities that I was expecting her to bring to the relationship. I had to do a little bit of work. But that's okay. Like I said, I was serious.

Gradually, I got through the list. I made sure I was everything I was expecting her to be. And suddenly, there she was. And now, here she comes.

Among the many attributes I wanted her to have were courage and self-reliance. I wanted her to be prosperous yet frugal. Prosperity includes wise stewardship of the gifts we receive. I did not go to my prayer cushion and declare to the Universe that I wanted a truck-driving momma with a couple of big dogs and a classic car. Those are the kinds of details I just don't think of. But this woman of my dreams has some ideas about things she wants to fix up in my—er, OUR—house, and when she was pricing movers, she felt that our money would be better spent on making the place a little more comfortable. She calculated that she could save a lot of money by trucking her possessions up here herself. So here she comes, ready or not, which leads to a whole other story.

I had to get ready for her. I'm 48 years old. I've lived alone for most of the past 16 years. A lot of stuff accumulates. To make matters worse, my accumulation of stuff was strewn all over the house. As a single guy, it didn't bother me at all that my dressers were filled with paperwork, mementoes and anything else I wanted out of sight. My clothes were just fine in laundry baskets next to the dryer. I had an intricate tabletop filing system with every horizontal surface reserved for its own type of correspondence. And you know . . . floors make great shelves. Some folks might not agree. But have you ever heard of anything falling off of the floor?

Suddenly, I'm not going to be living alone anymore. What worked for years is no longer an option. I have to use space more efficiently. So for the past week, I've been gathering, sorting, condensing and storing. I'm amazed at how big my house feels now. I have all kinds of empty space. It made me wonder why I didn't do this long ago. And the only answer I could come up with was perfectionism. I know that sounds strange. How could a perfectionist live like a slob? But perfectionism is an insidious disease.

When I was in high school, teachers, counselors and parents were always telling me that I was an underachiever. It was a trick. They thought that they could motivate me by stating the obvious. But I wasn't falling for it. I could clearly see what I needed to do in order to achieve my potential. But the things I was supposed to do could only be done haphazardly in the amount of time I had to do them. I didn't want to waste my time doing anything that wasn't done perfectly. And I thought that was really smart.

That's what makes perfectionism so insidious. It feels like genius, but it's not. Genius recognizes there is an underlying perfection in all things. Genius knows that perfection is dynamic, and to express perfection, we must be constantly changing. To discover perfection, we must be open to receiving and achieving new and different things. The perfect balance of nature is maintained by constant change. Stars burn. Planets hurtle through space and spin. Wind blows. Life grows, then dies and becomes food for new life. It's all perfect. And none of it does exactly what any perfectionist thinks it ought to do.

So the state of my house—before I rearranged everything—was a perfectionist's trick for procrastination. I didn't have everything I needed to make it conform to some weird notion of the right way to establish perfect order, so I let it become a static monument to inaction and imperfection. I could have written a country-western song about it: My shelves ain't perfect/ so my books are on the floor/ I'd go and get some whiskey/ but I don't drink it anymore/ cause it never done me no good neither . . ..

The blessing in my life right now is that perfection will not be denied. Change happens. And as I sat among my piles of clutter, I did my spiritual work. I changed my ideas about who I was and what my life should look like. I inventoried the corners of my mind and removed the old piles of baggage that kept me from embodying all of the qualities I was looking for in my right and perfect mate. And with the right inner changes, the right outer changes manifested perfectly.

So now my love is on the highway coming to her new home. She has all of the qualities I prayed for and more. The shape of my life is changing, and I can feel the perfection in it. This is a good thing.

THE RECURRING DREAM

I had a dream that I was a dog. That was peculiar. I've dreamt a lot of weird things in my life. My nights are filled with flying and monsters and supernatural powers. I've had epic dreams about conquering hoards of vicious marauders who were bent upon maiming me. I've had dreams of being naked in public and of being able to breathe under water. But in all of my wildest nighttime adventures, I was always myself—always a human who was shaped like and who acted like me. But the other night, I dreamed I was a dog.

I have dogs in my house now. They moved in last Tuesday. My cats are scandalized, and they've gone into hiding. The dogs have been sleeping under my bed. One of them is a border collie. She's bred for herding less intelligent animals; so naturally, she tries to protect me from everything she deems threatening. As I've spent the last week moving boxes and furniture, we've had several episodes of the border collie grabbing table legs, walls and pieces of cardboard with her teeth, and she snarls and snarfs and lets the offending item know that it better not try anything, or there will be hell to pay.

These have been busy days. I've gone to sleep exhausted on a few nights. I think I snore pretty loudly on those nights. It's what I'm told. And the other night, my snoring crested with snarling and snarfing. That's when I dreamt I was a dog. I was a border collie, and I was violently chewing a table leg. Then I woke up. The other dog—the golden retriever—woke me up by barking in my face. He didn't like the way I snarled and snarfed. He was telling me to knock off the racket.

This morning it felt good to go to work. I was going to a more familiar lack of control than I've been experiencing at home. Don't get me wrong. I love my new family. But it's so new and so different that going to work felt like a respite. As I was driving up the freeway, I heard a compelling ad on the radio. A woman said something like, "We all know that recurring dreams are the most significant ones, but have you ever noticed how many recurring dreams you have when you're awake?"

That jarred me into a whole new awareness. I had to turn the radio off and think about it. I had to notice what my mind was doing right at that moment. I knew I was going to work. I knew what projects awaited my attention, and I had a pretty good idea of who would be calling me and what they would be asking for. In some cases that was no big deal—even kind of pleasant. But there are always big issues, and there are always difficult people. And there's a part of my mind that always likes to rehearse conflicts and disagreements. That part of my mind always wants to prepare excuses or arguments. It's really bad spiritual practice because most of the problems I imagine never happen at all, and even if they do, the other people involved never know their lines. So all my mental preparation does is feed the Universe with negativity and invite the Universe to reflect that negativity back upon me.

All of the difficulty I expect at work is a recurring dream of my own making.

This evening walking out to my truck, the sunset was absolutely stunning. The low western sky was blue, with a long, thin, golden cloud stretching above the horizon. Above the golden cloud was another strip of blue, and above that, small, brilliant-pink clouds spread across dark, blue-gray sky. I had to stop and admire it. And when I did, I had one of those momentary mystical experiences of knowing that I was one with the beauty, one with the sky, and one with all creation. I did not BECOME one with the whole. I awakened to the truth that I am always one with the whole. And if I am always one with the whole of creation, I also must always be one with the Law of creation. The Law of creation is the creative mechanism of God. Whatever is in the Mind of God must become manifest as the body of God. And the body of God is the physical Universe.

So this morning as I was planning to have a particular experience at work, I was placing into the One Mind, of which I am part, the idea that certain people and certain issues would be difficult. Fortunately, the voice I heard on the radio rescued me from myself. When I was reminded that my life is a dream of my own making, I got busy making a new dream.

Every moment of life is brand new with the potential to be entirely different than any that has come before. But something inside us seeks familiarity. That is why many of our waking hours are spent having recurring dreams. But recurring dreams are the most significant. They tell us about ourselves. They reveal what we are clinging to—what we might want to consider letting go.

The recurring dream that has been my home life for the past few years is changing dramatically. I've gone from being a lonely bachelor to being surrounded by love. So I know that recurring dreams are not a life sentence. Usually they are just old habits of thought. Some recurring dreams are quite beautiful. There is no need to change them. But the ones that are distressing are really just a wake-up call. They are there trying to remind us that life is about growth and change.

This morning as I considered the recurring dream I have in the workplace, I knew it was time to create a new one. I chose a greater experience. And I got one. Today, I was invited to participate in a new project—completely unlike anything else I do on my job—completely unlike anything the company has ever done before. That's the way it works.

I had a dream that I was a dog. But I really wasn't a dog. And even in the dream, I didn't have a dog's mind. I had my own mind. My awareness and sense of self was the same as it is when I dream I'm naked in public or conquering vicious marauders or breathing under water. With my human mind, I observed that I had taken on the form of a border collie. I observed I was snarling and snarfing and attacking a table leg. But if the golden retriever hadn't woken me up, I'm sure I could have changed the dream. The only part of dreaming that is stable is the mind that is observing the dream—and the mind that is observing is also the mind that is creating the dream.

Tomorrow when I go to work, I can turn into a dog. I can snarf, snap and snarl at the furniture. I can bark. I could even pee on the floor. But I don't think I will. I'm living in my power right now. I see myself changing my dream. So this is a perfect time to change all of my dreams. My new dream for work is one of peace, harmony, creativity and joy. That is what I'm choosing. That is what I'm anticipating. The sunset I observed this evening was glowing with the beauty of creation. That same potential for that beauty is always present everywhere. It is present in me. It is present in you. We need only awaken to it. And I know we can—because we are wonderful. And so it is.

THE SPIRITUAL FOOTPRINT

I'm getting married.

This is big stuff. It's the real thing. I get dizzy just thinking about it. Part of me still can't believe it. So when I think about it, the part of me that knows it's true meets the part of me that can't believe it. It's like two powerful air masses moving in opposite directions. The point at which they meet begins to swirl. If I let the swirling gain momentum, a tornado is formed. I've found meditation to be extremely important lately. It calms the winds. It prevents psycho-tornadoes.

This is a rather violent image for something that is really wonderful—getting married. It is something that I've wanted for a long, long time—something that I prayed upon for a long, long time. But when we get what we want, it can be overwhelming. Nobody sits around and yearns for the little pleasures that barely cause a stir. When we dream, we dream big. And the Universe has a lot to give. The Universe is just waiting to give. We have only to be ready.

It took a long time for me to be ready. Even though I dreamed of being married—even though I prayed a long time to find my perfect partner—I was deeply entrenched in my consciousness of bachelorhood. My prayers said I wanted to be married, but my actions did not. I belonged to a twelve-step group that identified itself as being for singles. I bought season tickets for a theatre event that was billed for singles. I went to singles dances. I hooked up with some on-line matchmaking services—presumably for singles. I sought out single friends. I wrote on Monday nights about the challenges of loneliness. I wallowed in my singleness, so everything I was doing was telling the Universe that I was single. I gradually pulled back from those activities. I quit consciously cultivating my single identity. Suddenly, I recognized my fiancé. She'd been there all along. That's how prayer works. It's mostly a clearing away of untruth.

Now I'm engaged. I no longer wallow in singleness. I have my perfect sweetheart. She fills my time without dominating it. She makes me laugh. I'm never lonely anymore. My prayers have been answered, yet I still have my psycho-tornadoes. My dreams have come true, yet I still need to meditate frequently. An interesting discovery, now that I have what I wanted for so long, is that I'm still me. I still have old challenges—old demons. The thing that is most different is how I deal with them.

I had that single life down to a science. I could pretty much predict which issues were going to come up throughout the week. I knew what events would make me want to withdraw. I knew what situations would make me harsh and judgmental toward myself. I knew what aspects of my life made me feel guilty or inadequate. And as these challenges emerged, I knew all the right prayers, all the right affirmations, all the right activities and all the right strategies for addressing them. I grew proficient at dealing with me when there was only me to deal with.

Now there is someone else with me. My life is busier. It is less predictable. It is still seeking balance and structure. Amid that, familiar old feelings arise, and my first instinct is not to deal with them in the familiar old ways. It's spooky to see what comes up in my mind.

I'm not a blamer. I learned long ago that I get more respect when I own up to my shortcomings. I learned that things go more smoothly when I take responsibility for my mistakes. And my relationships remain harmonious when I let people make their own mistakes and deal with them in their own wonderful ways. That's the way I try to live in the world. And when I lived alone, anything that went wrong in the house—every mess, every misplaced item, every task left undone—was my doing. I was okay with all of it. I learned to be gentle and forgiving with myself. But now that I'm not alone, an unfamiliar voice has joined the chorus in my head. Suddenly if something is amiss, my first reaction is to blame. If there is a spot of juice spilled in the refrigerator, or one of those black science projects that tend to sneak into the vegetable drawer—if a door is left open or a light is left on—my first instinct is not to take full responsibility. My first thought is not about what I must do to make things better. The new voice in the chorus wants to blame, and this is quite alarming because it is blaming the most important person in my life.

I'm not saying that there is conflict. I've been good about recognizing that the blaming voice is not a voice of truth. I've stepped back from these reactions and sought greater ideas in my spiritual practice. My point is that no matter how spiritually grounded we are, when we get the big things we want, the conditions in our lives change, and we must use these changed conditions as opportunities to grow in the ways we apply our spiritual understanding.

I grew quite good at living alone, but living alone is not natural. We are all members of communities and societies. I lived alone, now I'm living in a family. A family is society in embryo. It is the place where I can take the attitudes and insights that I gained in my years of cultivating silence and begin expanding them to be a more positive presence on the planet.

When I was living alone, I took personal satisfaction in believing I lived harmony with all things. I always felt like I was being kind to the planet with my modest home and my small vehicle with a four-cylinder engine. I was careful to avoid being wasteful. I was proud that I didn't generate much garbage. Today, I had a bit of an eye-opener. I logged onto www.earthday.net and took a quiz that measured my "ecological footprint." It told me how much of the planet it took to sustain me in the lifestyle to which I am accustomed. It was rather disturbing to discover that ecologically, I'm an average American. I thought I was doing so well, but I learned that if everyone lived the way I do, it would require five planet earths to sustain us all. It made me consider that vast ecological footprint that is my life and the ways that I might reduce it. One of the things I can do is get married. Then I'm sharing my space and sharing my resources. But the concept of an ecological footprint made me think of more. Another idea I've been considering is my "spiritual footprint" and what that means during this time of tremendous change in my life.

Some people might argue that Spirit is infinite and indivisible, and because I am part of Spirit, my spiritual footprint is immeasurable. But I'm not convinced my influence is really that vast. I remember the days when I felt spiritually bankrupt. I felt powerless and victimized. I think my spiritual footprint was tiny then. It was only large enough to keep my heart beating and keep food in my mouth and a roof over my head. Over time, I've expanded my awareness—expanded my consciousness—and I've expanded my desire to be a positive force upon the planet. These spiritual and mental activities have broadened my spiritual footprint. There is no neat little quiz to tell me exactly how big my spiritual footprint is, and I'm sure it ebbs and flows. But I know it is vast. I attracted my perfect fiancé from hundreds of miles away. I feel connected to people on other continents. I feel compassion for people I will never meet. But having a vast spiritual footprint is not enough. The most important thing is how I fill that footprint.

I think that right now—right in this moment—I'm filling my spiritual footprint quite well. I've accepted love into my life, and I'm preparing for the next great adventure. I'm learning to share my space in the world. I'm learning that I still possess the capacity to blame, and I'm also learning I possess the capacity recognize that blaming only obscures truth. I'm learning to use my spiritual practice to clear it away. And the lessons I'm learning in my home are giving me tools I need to live better on the earth. With this expanded awareness—with greater spiritual, social and emotional tools—I can quiet my psycho-tornadoes. I can consciously reduce my ecological footprint. I can be more charitable with my resources and my attitudes, and I can clear away untruths that I might not have even seen before.

I'm getting married. It is a great spiritual gift to me. I intend to share the benefits with everyone everywhere by joining in a global consciousness of peace and harmony—because we are One. And we are wonderful. And so it is.

GOD IS IN THE CHOICES

Nine days until I get married. That will be April 30th—exactly 27 years since I enlisted in the Navy, exactly 21 years since the Navy set me free, and exactly 16 years since I decided I would no longer be a slave to drug and alcohol addictions. A numerologist could have all sorts of fun with this. I just see it as an easy way to remember my anniversary; otherwise, I tend to let days run together. I try not to give any one of them particular significance. Each one is an opportunity. Each one is another chance to change or grow my life in some wonderful new direction. This year, my new direction will be as a married man. It sounds like a good direction to me.

With this big change coming, I find myself having anxious moments. I'm not worried about any particular thing, but lots of little things loom and swirl just beyond my awareness. Sometimes I get little flashes of the enormity of this new commitment. Sometimes the busyness of getting prepared taps me on the shoulder. And I've been having lots of dreams at night about former girlfriends. Everything else that might be bothering me is less obvious, so I deal with it by turning my attention to God. It's a solution that is so simple that I almost feel like I'm cheating. But it gives me peace. It gives me strength.

And it reminds me that this marriage—this perfect marriage—is something that I prayed upon for a long time. We get what we want . . . as soon as we are ready.

In these final days of my protracted bachelorhood, I'm looking back upon the things I did to get ready. I see I could have been ready much sooner if I'd done things differently. And at the same time, I see that I would not be the man I've become if I had done things differently. I am the product of the choices I've made.

It feels good to say that—I am the product of the choices I've made. With vague and hidden anxieties looming just beyond the limits of my awareness, reminding myself that I'm the product of my own choices restores my sense of control. Much of my life has been spent discovering that I am not a victim. I guess it means I'm growing up.

"Growing up" can mean a lot of things. When I was 18, I felt grown up because I could drink legally. I went up and down Main Street every night checking in at all of the bars. I was looking for something, but I wasn't sure what it was. I think it was maturity. The bars were filled with adults. I thought they could teach me something. I learned to shoot pool and shake dice. I learned to drink shots. But that was the extent of it. I sure as hell didn't learn how to hold onto a job or how to save money. I learned how to find and take drugs, but I didn't learn how to distinguish friends from drug dealers. I got in enough trouble to keep things uncertain, but I didn't get enough trouble to want to change. Then one Sunday morning, I walked into a tavern with one of my friends. The usual customers were fatly planted in their usual places. They greeted my friend and me as we came through the door. In an unusual moment of awareness, I turned to my friend and said, "Let's go find something else to do. I don't want to become one of those people." My friend didn't know what I was talking about. But I knew it was time for change. It wasn't long after that I joined the Navy.

That change in conditions signaled a spiritual shift. Before I joined the Navy, I saw God as a cosmic disciplinarian with little mercy and less generosity. I believed there was a God, but I couldn't see that God doing anything but make people miserable. When I joined the Navy, I left the God I knew behind. I decided I would learn some discipline and some useful skills, and I felt like I was doing it myself. Those were the years that I felt God was unknowable. I had spiritual yearnings that I occasionally followed in my own private way, but I was careful not to ask God for anything because I felt it was a waste of time.

When I got out of the Navy, I still had my appetite for alcohol and drugs. The discipline I'd gained from my military training helped keep me under control for a time. But without reinforcement, the discipline eroded. That erosion took my last awareness of God with it. And I gradually became one of those people I'd tried to get away from years before. I was a slave to my addictions.

Addictions breed bad ideas. Bad ideas breed bad results. The situation I created made it necessary to seek help. Seeking help opened a new chapter in my spiritual development. It was the next step in my process of growing up.

When I went to the clinic where I would learn to grow sober, I wanted the express treatment. I wanted something fast—like a pill or a shot—that would shift the way I felt and thought and would give me the maturity and commitment I needed to live a healthy and happy life. The counselors laughed at me. They told me that I had a long and difficult task ahead of me, and the only help I would get would be from God. That was hard to take. I'd given up on asking God for anything so long before. But I was in a lot of pain, so I accepted a God that could give me strength when I was weak and comfort when I was uneasy. I must say I was surprised when that God came forth. As I accumulated days, then weeks, then months of a totally different life than I'd known before, I began expanding my faith. I added to the list of things I was willing to ask of God. As the list grew, so did the results. And as results increased, I began to grow up more.

There came a point at which I started wanting something that I'd never believed could be had. I wanted understanding. I wanted to know who or what God was, and I wanted to know why so many religions could have so many different answers. I wanted truth, and that was what I prayed for.

My prayers for truth led me to New Thought. Here's what I learned. Everything I ever believed about God was true. God is all there is, so God is whatever I need God to be at any given moment. When I thought God was merciless and stingy, God was exactly that. When I thought God was a cruel disciplinarian, God was exactly that. When I thought God was beyond my understanding, God was exactly that.

When I learned I needed God and believed It could give me strength and comfort, God gave me strength and comfort. When I became confident enough to pray for courage, God gave me courage. Every gift I felt certain that God could provide was mine when my faith was complete. So when I prayed for truth—knowing I would find it—whole worlds of awareness became available to me. But the most important thing I learned was to quit thinking about what I didn't want to be and start thinking about what I wanted to be. My sobriety came by a slow and indirect route because I only knew what I did not want to be. After studying New Thought, I decided I wanted to be married. I decided it had to be with someone who understood me and supported me on my spiritual journey. I made choices that supported that goal. Now it is about to happen.

As I prepare to accept the gift of marriage, which the Universe arranged with absolute skill, I'm looking at what God is to me now. It's almost astounding. I see and feel the power and presence of God in every aspect of my life. I know God in the love that I feel. I hear God in the laughter of my beloved. I feel God in the sloppy wet kisses that I get from the dogs. I feel God in the purring of the cats when I pick them up to cuddle. I taste God in the food upon my table. I'm surrounded by God in the support I'm receiving from loving family and friends. But most of all—my greatest connection to God—is in the choices that I make. God is present in my life. God responds to my prayers by providing new opportunities every day. But the most dramatic results to all of my prayers occur when I make good choices.

As I deal with the feelings and events that are surrounding my marriage, I continually remind myself that everything that is happening is the result of a choice that I have made. I have chosen to be the man I've become, and God supports me in my choices because I know that is what God does. In this most recent spiritual step of knowing God as my own choices, I'm preparing for marriage by asking myself a simple question. Through all of the changes and in all my activities, I ask myself, is the person you are right at this moment contributing to the person you intend to become?

This moment is saturated with God, and God brings the opportunity for a myriad of choices. If I intend to be lean and healthy, I can choose activities and behaviors that contribute to that result. If I intend to be prosperous and comfortable, I can make choices that contribute to that as well. Right now the most important thing to me is to be a loving husband. As God is in my choices, I can elect attitudes and behaviors that contribute to creating the result I desire. So I'm going to go do that—right now—because my fiancé is wonderful, and so are you. And so it is.

BEYOND IDEAS OF GOD

Here's one for you. If it can't be put into words, can it still be an idea? I think it can. I think language is great for examining, refining, and sharing ideas. But I think most ideas begin somewhere outside the realm of words. I have this preverbal notion about God that I wish I could convey in its purity. But the closest I could come to that would be to send a blank page. And rather than read what it says, I think most people would project onto it whatever meaning they suppose I was trying to convey.

Maybe that would be perfect. Every one could project an idea of God. It could be the beginning of hundreds of new religions. And each one would be just as good as any of the religions already going. In fact, they would probably be better.

My wife is fond of saying "God is greater, grander and more magnificent than any religion that tries to explain it, including our own." One of the things she means when she says it is that our ideas about God are all incomplete.

Perhaps they didn't begin that way. Perhaps the original idea behind every religion was a perfect flash of absolute inspiration. But then the person who had the flash of inspiration tried to share it, and it all got lost in translation. That would explain why sacred texts are all long and rambling. That would explain why my musings are long and rambling. Every attempt to talk about God falls short, yet the one doing the explaining keeps trying. Eventually, a lot of words are flying around. Some people try to nail down a few of the most important words. They call them truth and make them into rules. Depending upon which words they choose as most important, those people might be the faithful or the superstitious. They might become beacons of light, or they might become fundamentalists. Most of them fall somewhere in between. And then there are some people who let the swirl of words create a sense of something greater. Those are the mystics.

My mother tells me that when I was a very little boy, I talked to trees. I didn't sit and lecture them. I sat and shared ideas with them. She told me this when I was in my twenties. I was high on pot and rambling about how I liked imagining that the earth contained all the ideas that the people who lived on it ever thought. I liked imagining that the trees were like thought antennas that captured our thoughts and sent them down through their roots into the earth, and if we could raise our sensitivity, we could actually get the trees to reveal those thoughts back to us. And that was when she told me about my history with trees. "Your grandfather talked to them too." she said. She wasn't high on pot.

I eventually quit talking with trees and started talking with people. For several years, I forgot what the trees knew and started learning words. Those words translated into knowledge as well as superstition. I learned facts and I learned lies. I had to sort them all out. Sometimes it was easy. I remember walking along as my mother took my sister to and from her first few days of kindergarten. I was only four. The bigger kids told me, "Step on a crack; you break your mother's back." For several steps I tried to avoid the cracks in the sidewalk. But it occurred to me that I'd never before tried to avoid cracks. Before I heard the rhyming words, they simply were not an issue. I stepped intentionally on a crack, and my mom pretended it hurt. But I could tell she was okay. That was my first conscious experience with superstition. But as time went on, the superstitions I learned became harder to disprove.

Of course, now I'm talking about religious superstition. I went to Sunday school every week. I learned the tenets of the religion of my grandparents. When I tried to gather details—when I tried to assemble evidence—I was told to believe it or go to Hell. That sounded a lot like "Step on a crack; you break your mother's back."

When I was twenty-five, I was in the Navy, and my ship was in dry-dock in Bremerton, Washington. I was away from my familiar homeport of San Diego. I was lonely. At that time, there were billboards all around town that said, "I Found It." It was the beginning of an ad campaign. The billboards were meant to be teasers. I was supposed to wonder what the billboard creators found that was so great. But I knew that the next phase was going to be about salvation. The billboards were effective in that I started thinking about God. But rather than running off to Sunday services, I tried gathering spiritual information that challenged the traditions I grew up with. I didn't know where to look. I picked around in used bookstores. I tried the library. I found enough information to feel comfortable believing that traditions and popular notions about God were mostly horseshit. I amused myself thinking how my old Sunday school teachers would be offended hearing me use the words "God" and "horseshit" in the same sentence. But something within me was not being satisfied.

One warm Friday evening, I knew my friends were gathering for another long night of drinking beer. I had my reefer in my pocket, and I would have normally joined them. But an inner longing took hold of me. I gathered up my I Ching, a pocket-sized New Testament that I'd been dragging around since boot camp, an old philosophy textbook from the Purple Heart Veterans' Thrift Store, and an anthology of religious texts from the shipyard library. I bought a bottle of red wine and drove to a park at the edge of town. I carried my pot and my wine and my books to the top of a hill where I found a small clearing with a large flat rock beside the trail.

I carefully arranged my things on the rock. I didn't have a plan, but I wanted a new idea about God. I took a few puffs of pot and a few sips of wine. Then I reverently arranged some rocks and sticks to make a small shrine. I did it without a plan. I let the forest decide how it should look. When the shrine felt complete, I sat for a while and listened to it. I wanted a flash of insight or inspiration that would give meaning to my young life. I had a few more sips of wine. I then mustered up all the faith I could find—superstition perhaps—that if I closed my eyes and flipped open one of my books, I would be led by Divine Mystery to exactly the passage I needed to read. I carefully read a page from The Pre-Socratics. I carefully read a page from the New Testament. The anthology of religions opened to a passage from some Hindu literature. Finally, I tossed three coins to select a passage from the I Ching.

When I finished my readings, I silently reflected upon the fact that nothing I read had made a whit of sense to me. The passages taken out of context without background were meaningless. The reading from the I Ching was an impenetrable metaphor. Yet for all my lack of understanding, I felt oddly fulfilled. My intention that evening was to be with God. Somehow, it worked. The sun set behind a distant hill. The park started growing dark. I went back to town to find my friends, but I was different.

Usually Friday nights on the town were a frantic scramble to find something outside myself to fill the void in my heart. I drank lots of beer, smoked lots of grass, and tried to chase any women that were bold enough to frequent the sailor bars. These activities never satisfied me—because we can never get enough of what we don't need in the first place. But that night after inventing my own private little ritual, I was strangely at peace. I didn't need anything. I was happy to be among my friends.

It would be twenty years before I happened into New Thought. By then my life would have a completely different shape. I would have different values and different priorities. The pot and the wine and the Navy would all be part of my past. The thing that did not change was my desire to have a relationship with God that was meaningful to me. I never repeated the ceremony that I did in the Washington forest. But I did keep my heart open to the possibility that I might someday find a religion that didn't sound like superstition.

In New Thought, I've found a spiritual home. I've learned that God is always listening and responding. I've learned that God can be whatever I need God to be at any given moment because God is everywhere and in everything all the time. And I've learned it is okay to believe that God speaks to me in ways that are beyond my understanding. When I use words to talk about God, I risk limiting God. But I also know that it's okay to honor the mystery in whatever manner suits me in the moment.

I'll never fully understand what happened in my forest ceremony. Perhaps I just needed to be alone. Maybe it was just the wine. But maybe too there was a communication that took place. Perhaps as I read the pages that I didn't understand, something inside me was hearing the spirit in which the words were written. Or maybe as my brain failed to decipher the words on the page, my intention was busily opening my heart to the whispers of God. This is something I can never know. But I can know that investing time in sacred ceremony—even without a religion to go with it—made a difference that night. And so it is.

ABOUT THE AUTHOR

R. Scott de Snoo is a pulpit minister, a recovering alcoholic, a storyteller, a computer technician, a writer and a mystic living and working in Southeastern, Wisconsin.

What a man is and does in the world cannot predict the level of impact and the sphere of influence that he unwittingly wields on opinion leaders, educators and organizations. Scott's deeply personal essays have been used by ministers, leaders, teachers and individuals all over the country to move more deeply into asking themselves questions of self discovery—questions that both dim and fuel their faith, inspire their callings and impact lives beyond their own.

Scott's inner authority comes not from his unique and enviable childhood led in a "Leave it to Beaver" setting in Waukesha, WI, nor from his experience as a needle-using methamphetamine addict, or as a drunk, though all those experiences helped Scott discover that neither who he is nor who he was have anything to do with what is going on outside of himself.

Scott spent six years in the peacetime Navy, working, brawling, and learning, and discovering the world beyond Wisconsin. When he returned to the hard work of rebuilding a sober life and graduating with honors from the University of Wisconsin, the writer and the mystic began to emerge.

And everywhere Scott went, the world was his mirror. And everything he has learned about his nature is your nature. And everything he has recorded about his story is your story.

More about Scott and Lisa de Snoo and about
Spiritual Living of Greater Milwaukee can be found at
www.rsgm.net

To find information about other New Thought churches,
centers, groups and ministers around the world, check at
www.antn.org
and
www.unitedcentersforspiritualliving.org